WALKS IN SOUTHERN POWYS
& THE BORDERS

WALKS IN SOUTHERN POWYS & THE BORDERS

by
Andrew Johnson

With original drawings
by
Jenny Kirk

LOGASTON PRESS 1991

LOGASTON PRESS
Little Logaston Woonton Almeley
Herefordshire HR3 6QH

First published by Logaston Press 1991
© Andrew Johnson 1991

ISBN 0 9510242 8 0

Set in Baskerville 10/12 pt by Logaston Press
and printed in Great Britain on Five Seasons 100 per cent
recycled paper by Ebenezer Baylis and Son, Worcester

Contents

INTRODUCTION

Welcome to 35 walks in southern Powys and the borders.

Each walk is on definitive footpaths and bridleways with as little road as is compatible to make an accessible walk in each part of the countryside. On some walks churches, earthworks or villages are included and often information about these is given.

All the walks have been walked in the 18 months prior to publication, and any comments about awkward places have been included in the preamble to each walk. In many cases I have reported these problems to the relevant county council, so it may be that no problems will in fact exist, though I fear they still will.

The number of the walk relates to the number on the location map. An estimate of the length of time the walk takes is then given. This time only allows for walking at a reasonable pace and not for stopping to admire the view, or to identify all the wayside plants!

There then follows a note about the walk together with some information on the condition of the paths and tracks to be taken. In the descriptions I use 'path' to describe either a well marked route only wide enough to walk along, or where there is no clearly defined route, for example across or alongside fields. 'Track' refers to a well defined wide route, in all probability used by farm vehicles.

Then follows a description of how to reach the walk's start point by vehicle from the nearest town or large village. The symbol ℗ on each map indicates the location of the suggested parking place.

The walk itself is then described and the written directions should be read in conjunction with the sketch map provided. I also recommend use of an Ordnance Survey map of the 1:50 000 series to help identify views. The relevant map number and co-ordinates for the start point of each walk are given above the walk's title.

I cannot guarantee that the countryside remains unchanged, so you may find, for example, that some hedgerows have been grubbed up, or that additional fences have been erected and some paths obstructed.

Finally, my thanks go to Jenny Kirk for her drawings and to Steve Wolstencroft for drawing the maps.

LOCATION MAP FOR WALKS

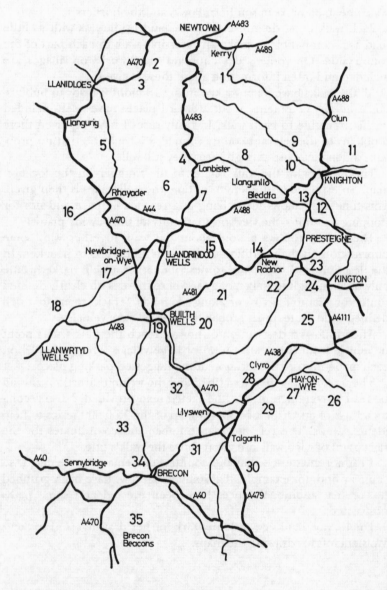

LIST OF WALKS

WALKING LAW AND CODES

General

On a public path the public has a right of access on foot only, and on bridleways a right of access on horse and pedal cycle as well. On each you can take a 'natural accompaniment' which includes a dog, prams and pushchairs. All dogs should be kept under close control, and always on a lead when near livestock. Some public paths are way-marked by the landowner, and have coloured arrows at junctions and changes in direction to indicate the course of the path. The colours are usually yellow for footpaths and blue for bridleways. The highway authority, being the relevant County Council in this area, has a duty to signpost footpaths where they leave a metalled road. There is no time limit in which to fulfill this duty, and in addition signposting can be considered unnecessary in certain limited circumstances. In effect, most paths are neither signposted nor waymarked.

Maintenance

County Councils have a duty 'to assert and protect the rights of the public to the use and enjoyment' of paths and 'to prevent as far as possible the stopping up or obstruction' of such paths. It is normally the surface of the path that belongs to the Council, the soil underneath belonging to the landowner who adjoins the path.

Owners of the land have the primary duty of maintaining stiles, though the Council must contribute a quarter of the cost and can contribute more if they wish.

Often County Councils have agreements with District or Parish Councils whereby the latter maintains the path and charges the County Council; but any complaint about non-signposted, unmaintained or obstructed paths should be sent to the County Council,

and can also be sent to the Ramblers Association who may pass it
onto a local group to follow up.

Obstructions

If the path crosses a field, the field may be ploughed and planted,
but the farmer must make good the surface of the path within two
weeks of starting to plough, or if prevented by exceptional weather
conditions, as soon as possible thereafter. Reinstatement now has a
legal definition under the Rights of Way Act 1990. Minimum widths
apply to definitive footpaths and bridleways across and along the
edges of fields (1 metre's width is the minimum for a cross field footpath, those for other categories are wider still). In addition landown-
ers should remove overhanging vegetation which may inconvenience
a walker or prevent the line of the footpath from being apparent on
the ground.

If you come across an obstruction on a path, so long as you are a
bona fide traveller, in other words if you haven't set out with the
specific purpose of removing the obstruction, you're entitled to
remove it, but should only remove as much as is necessary to pass
through. Alternatively if there is an easy way round the obstruction,
you may legally take that route, and would have a defence to any
charge of trespass.

Legal action against the landowner lies essentially in the hands of
the County Council, and they can prosecute or enter onto the land,
carry out the necessary work and reclaim the costs involved. Thus, in
case of persistent problems, the information should be passed on to
the County Council.

Bulls

It is illegal to keep bulls of a recognized dairy breed (Ayrshire,
British Friesian, British Holstein, Dairy Shorthorn, Guernsey, Jersey
and Kerry breeds) in fields crossed by a public path, except in open
hill areas or if they are under ten months old. Nor is it legal to keep
any other bulls in such fields unless accompanied by cows or heifers.

If owners disregard the law relating to bulls and thereby endanger
the public, an offence may be committed under the Health and
Safety at Work Act 1974, and the police may institute proceedings.

Trespass

If you stray off a path you may be trespassing which is a civil wrong, not a criminal offence, and the landowner may have a remedy in damages and/or an injunction. If you are trespassing solely as a way of avoiding a blockage on a path, then you automatically have a defence.

If you are unsure of your route, remember always to be polite and find out where you should be walking.

Definitive Footpath Maps

The County Council is required to keep a definitive map of footpaths. Ordnance Survey maps may show additional paths and it is these, often still public rights of way, which are most likely to be obstructed or overgrown. It is also more difficult to follow the exact line of paths on the larger scale maps as field boundaries are not shown. Copies of definitive footpath maps can be obtained, usually at a price, from the relevant County Council. In the old county of Herefordshire, the maps can be inspected at Hereford library. In Powys, inspection can be made at County Hall in Llandrindod Wells, and in Shropshire at the Council Offices in Ludlow.

All paths on definitive footpath maps are public rights of way and to show that a path is on such a map is sufficient to establish a legal right of passage. To incorporate paths onto the definitive map it is necessary to prove that the path has been dedicated to public use. This can happen by either act or omission—either the landowner may simply grant the public the right of way, or, alternatively and more likely, you must provide evidence that the public have used the route for at least twenty years without an actual or implied prohibition by the landowner. Applications for additions to the map as well as reports of obstructions should be addressed to the relevant County Council.

Once established a right of way does not 'disappear' simply through lack of use, though this may provide evidence in support of an application to extinguish a path. It is normally the County or District Council who will make an application to extinguish or divert a path, and a publicity and consultation process has to be followed before the order may be confirmed or rejected.

Country Code

Remember when walking to take other peoples' interests in the land into consideration, and remember that you only have the right to walk along the footpaths and not to, for example, use them to carry wood from adjoining land. Remember especially to:

1. Keep any dogs under close control, and you are required to keep a dog on a lead when in a field with livestock. Take additional care at lambing time which normally runs from Christmas to the end of April. If your dog does worry sheep, you may find that not only is it shot, if that is the only way the farmer can stop it, but you may also have to compensate the farmer for any damage it has caused.

2. Leave gates as you find them—remember you may close off livestock from water by closing a gate meant to be open. Always close a gate you've opened to pass through. If it is impossible to open a gate climb over at the hinged end to minimalize the risk of damaging the gate.

3. Always keep to a path unless it is easier to avoid an obstruction by leaving it, which you are entitled to do.

4. Never light fires, and extinguish all matches and cigarettes.

5. Take your litter home.

6. Leave livestock, crops and machinery alone.

7. Make no unnecessary noise.

8. Protect wildlife, plants and trees—remember it may be an offence to damage certain plants and wildlife. It is a simple rule—if you leave them alone they may be there next time for others to look at.

KERRY RIDGEWAY

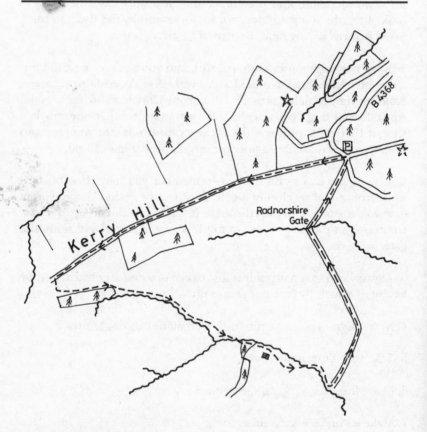

One and a half hours.

A walk largely on tracks and some paths, with two awkward fences to cross. There are wide views to the north from the ridgeway, whilst other sections of the walk involve passing alongside small streams, or walking over open hillside.

From the village of Kerry head south on the road which joins the B4368 Clun road. Turn right onto this and drive uphill till you reach the summit where you can park in a car park-cum-picnic area on the left, in a space set in front of a forestry plantation.

14

The walk starts on the other side of the B road, passing through the gate and then taking the right-hand track which traverses the ridgeway. You soon pass a forestry plantation on your right, and further on, one on your left. Beyond this second plantation the track starts to genty drop towards a small cleft in the ridge. Just before you reach the low point you come to a gateway, and here, though the definitive path carries on and then doubles back, you want to turn left and walk up the fence on your right—this is to avoid having to cross this fence where no gate or stile is provided. When you are some thirty yards in front of the next small wood, bear left and head towards the far corner of this wood, crossing one awkward fence in the process. Once over this head for the gate just to the left of the corner of the wood. Once through this bear slightly further right and walk across this field to a gate on the far side.

This gate leads onto a track which follows the course of a small stream flowing out from the hillside on your right. Keep to this track and, below a narrow tongue of wood ahead, it fords the stream and passes through a stock handling area. In the field beyond this head to the immediate left of a derelict barn and cottage on the far side of the field (on much the same line as you've been walking), turning through the gateway on the far side of the cottage. Here the path follows the top of the bank above the stream and the boggy ground surrounding it, heading for some trees that project into the field. As you near these you'll see that they are the old hedges that marked the sides of a track, and you follow these down to the stream, making the second awkward fence crossing to reach the stream.

Ford the stream, and bear right on the paths on the other side so as to cling to the banks above the stream, following it round into a wider more open area. As the stream enters this area it makes a small waterfall. On the corner with the wood on the far side of this area, turn left up a track. (This is not a definitive path, but as one definitive bridleway leads to it and nowhere else, I think it a fair presumption that this track can be walked.)

Keep to this track, it bending to the left as it becomes adjacent to the ends of the fields on your left. Still keep to it as it crosses the hillside and then drops down to cross a stream. Here a definitive path leads off across the field on the far side to the top left-hand corner of the field, where you join your old route. However, it would seem preferable to keep to the track and walk back to the gate opposite which you've parked, and I can't but help think that this would in fact cause the farmer less concern in any event.

LLANDINAM

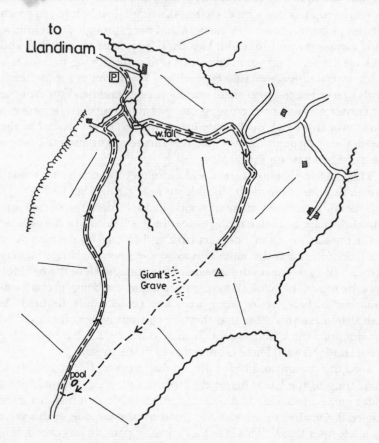

One and a quarter hours.

A walk largely on tracks, though one vanishes for a while, in the hills above the Severn valley. There are wide views which are well worth the not overly strenuous ascent.

In Llandinam, on the A470 just south of Newtown, turn away from the Severn on the little road by the post office. Keep on the most main little road, which will lead round to the right, then left and up towards the hills. Keep on tarmac till it comes to an end at an old quarry on the right, where you can park. (If you reach a gate closed across the road, you can drive on through—just remember to close the gate after you.)

From the quarry walk on up the track which is a continuation of the road, keeping right at the first split which occurs almost immediately. This will bring you round to a stock handling area where you keep left at another division of the ways, shortly to turn left once more and cross a little bridge. Once you've made the turn, you can look out for a small waterfall on your right.

Keep on this track, and it will wind its way up the hill to a corner of fencing, before turning right and passing by another small quarry. Keep to this track and after a few wiggles it will settle down and follow a fence on your left. Near the summit of the hill it passes through another gate. Here the track turns slightly to the right and loses some of its stoned surface, making it more gentle to walk on. The track soon descends very slightly to cross a small dip in the hillside, and in this dip you carry on on a grassy track straight ahead, whilst the more main track turns left and drops down the hillside. In this dip you pass through the line of a small earthwork called the Giant's Grave, which probably marked a territorial boundary.

You now carry on walking across the side of the hill for quite some distance. The grassy track soon crosses a boggy patch of ground below a Mountain Ash and passes through another gate. Take a moment here to observe the track's course ahead, for it soon all but disappears. When it does, still keep walking on the same line, and you start to pass some rushy areas to your right. When you seem to be about adjacent to the highest part of the hill, turn right and cross over it towards a fence you'll see almost on the summit. You should also come to a pool—if you don't, bear left before you reach the fence until you do, and pass round the pool's left where you'll join another track towards the corner of the field and which leads you to a gate in the fence. Once through this gate, turn right on the track.

You'll now gain wide views to the west as the track follows the fence for a while, then diverges from it. Shortly after this the track splits, and you keep tp the left-hand route. Further on this in turn splits, and you keep to the right-hand track, following the hillside down. This will soon join with the other track, but is technically the course of the definitive footpath. Keep to the track, turning right at the junction with the drive to a house, and it will lead you back to the stock handling area. Turn left here to return to your vehicle.

Y FOEL

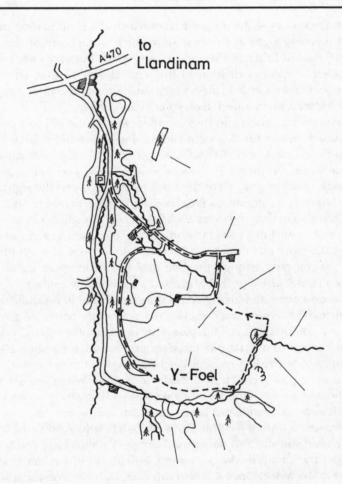

One and a quarter hours.

This walk takes its name from a strange semi-barren hill around which you walk. There is a lovely stream to shadow at one point and it is a very pleasant walk. However, beware. One of the paths is fairly overhung and requires a lot of ducking, and another passes through some recent forestry plantations, making for very hummocky and tough going. It is quite a short walk, but arduous in its own way.

From Newtown on the A470 you pass through Llandinam, and take the first minor road off to the left after a couple of miles or so and opposite a stone built house with a plaque which states 'This house was erected Anno Dom 1832'. Drive down the road, bearing left at the first split, cross the stream and parking at the second split.

Walk up the left-hand road, and turn right up the farm drive for Glynfach. As you enter the farmyard, go through the gate on your immediate left, and then follow the fence on your right round the vegetable garden and up to the top corner of the field. Here you cross out via the stile. Turn right onto the track, and keep on the old track downhill when the newer track bears left into a field.

Keep on the old track, which soon swings left, crosses a field and enters some woodland. Keep on this through the woodland. When the track narrows and starts to become slightly overgrown, look out for a fence set below the bank to the right of the path. There is a clear section of bank where this is quite visible and where you walk down the bank to this fence, and then turn left along it. The path is quite clear for a while, but then becomes obstructed by overhanging branches. Keep going, and when the way seems blocked by a fir tree, don't give up, you're almost in the clear! Force your way past the tree and once over the fence behind, again follow the fence on your right, but in clearer country. Further on the path diverges from the fence on your right to cross a shoulder of the hill so as to join the stream flowing down its other side. Here you seem to have Africa up high to the left, and Scotland to the right! Over the shoulder the path, which you have to keep observing closely to always ascertain its route, drops down towards the stream in the little valley, eventually following a new fence and a dilapidated wall beyond which the stream lies.

Ahead you cross a stile and then the stream itself, soon to recross the stream and another stile into a wood. Keep to the right-hand path in the wood and once out of the mature wood, keep to its edge, between it and some more young plantations. At the end of the mature wood on your left, you stay much to the same line, keeping to a wide 'track' left within the plantations. This leads you along the hillside, and once over the slight rise in the ground, you'll see a gate on the far side of the plantation at the end of the 'track'. Cross this gate and turn right on the track beyond it.

Follow this track to the lane ahead, on which you turn left to return to your vehicle.

19

LLANANNO

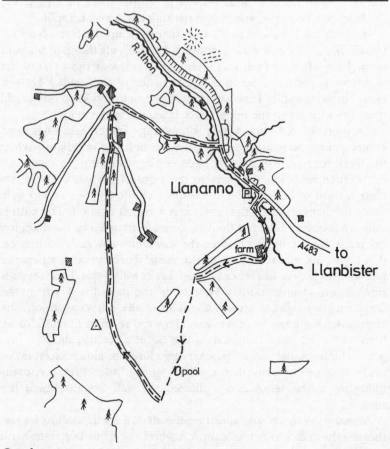

R. Ithon

Llananno P

farm

A483 to
Llanbister

pool

One hour.

A walk largely on tracks with wide views over the countryside
obtained from a narrow ridge along which part of the walk is made.
There is a fairly short section of very minor road, and an even
shorter stretch of A road which has wide verges. Also included is
Llananno Church, which is well worth a visit to see its rood screen.

Heading north from Crossgates on the A483, pass by Llanbister and
just before the A road reaches a cutting on the right, look out for the

sign to Llananno Church by the roadside on the left. The church itself is a small building set down from the road. You can park in the lay-by opposite the cutting and beyond the church.

Go through the gate at the start of the lay-by which also leads to the church. It is not known when the church was founded, but it was rebuilt in 1877, when the rood screen was dismantled and stored, being re-erected when the church was completed. It was slightly lengthened and re-modelled to fit the new church, with the western niches being filled with carvings of biblical figures. Below and above are vines, representing Good, as recorded in Verse 1, Chapter 1 of St. John's Gospel 'I am the vine and my Father is the husbandsman.' This symbolism was strenthened when wine, the product of the vine, was drunk at the Last Supper in remembrance of Christ's blood.

The walk goes down the track and over the bridge across the Ithon, after which the track bears left and leads up to a farm. Walk through the yard, passing out by the gate to the left of the house. Through the gate keep to the track to the right which leads uphill, then turns right and leads across the hillside. This then follows a little stream on the right to a gate. Through this gate you emerge onto an open hillside, where the path is indistinct for a while. The best route appears to be to head along the fence on your right till you come to a gate from which a large track leads downhill. Here turn more to the left and ascend the knob of the hill. As you rise up this, you'll see a little dip between the knoll you're on and another over to the left. You want to aim for the far side of the top of this dip where you'll come to a pool, or dried out pan—depending upon the weather. From this pool you join tracks once more. Take the track down the far side of the hill from the pool and you'll come to a junction of routes in the sadddle below.

Here you turn sharp right on a track which leads back uphill and round the head of a little cwm. This track is waymarked and leads you to the right of the spot height, beyond which you walk along the crest of a narrow ridge, soon to gently descend the hillside. This track later enters the remains of some very old woodland, at the foot of which it emerges on to a lane. Turn left on this and it leads you down to the minor road.

Turn right on the minor road, and right again when you reach the main road, to return to your vehicle.

NANTGWYN

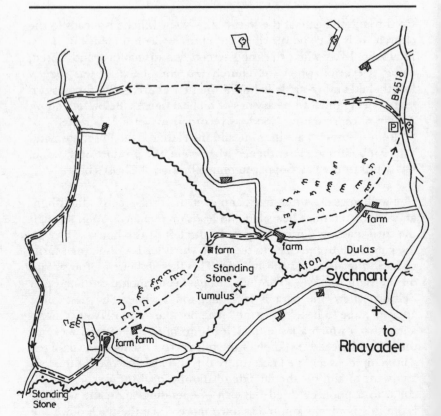

One and three-quarter hours.

A walk largely on tracks or by field boundaries around gentle hills to the north of Nantgwyn. Two standing stones are passed, along with rocky outcrops, and there are wide views towards the south. The walk is generally fairly level, though there are a few small clambers.

From Rhayader take the B4518 north to St. Harmon. Stay on the B road through St. Harmon and then through the small hamlet of Nantgwyn. The road then crosses a stream, bends to the left and rises till it meets a small wood on the right. You want to park opposite this wood where a track leads off through a gate.

Walk up this track which soon bends to the left near a small wood and then slowly rises up the hillside to pass to the left of a cottage set in some trees. Beyond this the track comes to an end, but the path follows the fence on your right in the same direction over the hillside. Further on you pass the end of a narrow strip of conifer shelter belt, not far beyond which you once more join a track. This swings slightly to the left and you soon come to a crossroads of tracks.

Turn left at this junction, and this track slowly curves to the right. It eventually splits, the main track heading off to the left down a valley towards a farm. However you stay on the right-hand smaller track, this crossing the ridge of the hill, and then, as you start to descend towards a boggy looking patch of ground this side of a large conifer plantation, the track swings left through a gateway. Here you initially follow the young shelter belt and fence on your left, but the track then swings through the field to join the corner of another field down the slope. Once more it becomes a more obvious track, and you follow the fence on your right down to a metalled lane this side of the river in the valley below. Turn left on this lane, and you'll quickly come to the first standing stone in the field on your right.

Follow the lane round the hill on your left, rising to the farm ahead. Pass the barns on your right, but before you reach the farmhouse itself, go through the gate on the left onto the track which leads round behind it. Keep on ahead in the yard, passing to the left of all the buildings excepting one barn on your left, to a gate into the field beyond. Turn right through this gate and follow the stoned track to the gate at the end. Through this, keep following the wall and fence on your right above the next farm through a gorsey patch further along and then via a gate above another farm. (It is whilst passing round this farm that you need to look out for the second, larger standing stone in the middle of a field off to the right.) At the end of the bank above this farm, turn right between the house and the barns, and head down the track straight down the hillside.

This track will lead you to the next farm, once you've crossed a small stream. Immediately before you would enter the yard of this farm, you turn left up the side of the wall and once more keep a boundary on your immediate right and the open hillside on your left. You will pass through a few more gates, and above another farm after which the path and boundary line bends more to the left. You will eventually emerge into a field above the wood near where you parked. Walk across this field to the left of the far corner to leave it by the gate onto the track on which you started out.

ABBEYCWMHIR

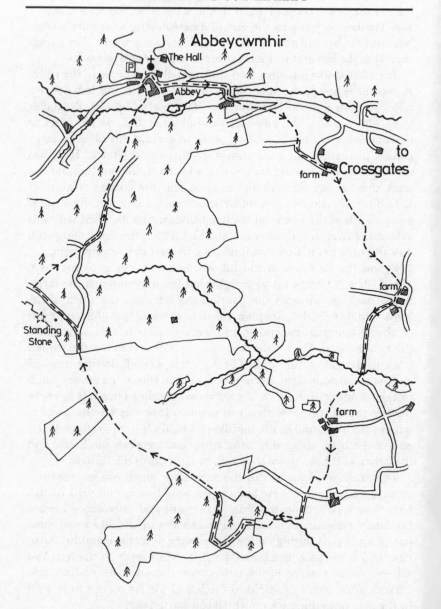

Two and a quarter hours.

A walk on a mixture of tracks and paths through fields, open hillside and some conifer plantation, though the route through this is more varied than can often be the case. The remains of Abbeycwmhir Abbey can be seen towards the end of the walk. There are some fences to cross, though at most of these points there is either a helpful post or tree or an absence of barbed wire.

Park at the church in Abbeycwmhir.

With your back to the church turn left on the road, and follow it round past The Hall on the left, and over the brook in the valley bottom. As you make the turn to the left once over the brook, go through the first gate on the right into the field to the left of the cottages. Walk diagonally across this field, to a point just below the top far corner. Here you come to a stile leading to a path through the wood. Cross the new track on the far side of the wood and the stile on the other side of the track. Then follow the line of the old track sloping across this field and through a gateway into the next. In this second field, it turns slightly more to the right, joins a fence at an internal corner of the field and then leaves it via a gateway onto a track hedged on both sides. Follow this track across a little gully, after which it bends left once more and leads above some barns to a farm. Walk through the farmyard on the track, through which it bends to the right. Immediately beyond all the buildings you come to a collection of gates into several fields. The track itself swings left once more and descends the hill, but in front of you are two gates, one to either side of a hedge which rises slightly uphill. Take the right-hand gate and follow this hedge over the ridge to a gate in the corner of the field.

Here you turn slightly more to the left, the old track passing between a couple of trees as it heads downhill to the stream below, following a bank on your left to the stream itself. You should meet the stream just to the left of a fence on the far side which leads away uphill. Cross the stream and its associated fence to the left of this other fence, and then follow it uphill to the corner of the field. Turn left in front of the fence at the top, soon to meet another slightly awkward fence crossing. From here the route improves once more. Keep following the hedge and fence on your right, passing through the fields and you'll approach another farm. Go through the gates here and once you meet the track on the near side of the farm, turn right on it. This will lead you above the farm buildings, including one large new shed, all the time roughly keeping to the contour of the hill. The track will lead out into a field some way past the buildings, and then it drops down to cross the next stream. Once over this, don't stay on the track, but bear half right and pick up the line of an old field boundary which almost aims at the next farm on the slope above. In the corner of this field, go round the end of the fence on your left, and keep on the line of the old fence you were following across the next field and up the bank on the far side. This should lead you to a track which itself leads up to a gate to the field between the bank and this next farm.

Once through the gate, don't take the new track, but bear slightly right across the field to the gate to the right of the new barns and so into the farmyard. Bear right in the farmyard to pass to the right of the barn which stands rather in the middle of it. This will lead past it and onto a track leading off the far side of the yard and to the right of the house. Keep on this track and it will lead you across the next fields towards a small new barn. Turn right in front of this and follow the track round the edge of the rough ground in which the barn stands. At the far corner you'll come to a collection of gates, and you turn right into a long thin field which runs up past the corner of the conifer wood. Walk across to a point just below the conifer wood. Above a stream you'll come to the signs of an old gateway—there may even be part of the gate still there. As you can guess the next short section of path is not in an ideal state! Cross the fence at this gateway, then shadow the stream on your left, crossing a feeder ditch and when you come to the next ditch, where the trees have been lopped off and some re-digging has been done, follow this up to the conifer wood. On the far side of the fence at the edge of the wood you should see a track leading into the wood. You've guessed it—you need to cross this fence and then follow the track.

This soon bends sharp left before swinging more gently right, though here you may want to take the path on the bank above the track to avoid becoming too water-logged. When you reach the far end of the wood, turn right on the track up the side of the field, still inside the woodland. This track will lead up the hillside, before turning left and leading you up and later across the hillside to lead you out on the far side of the wood. Here you turn left on the track which follows the wood on your left and then a fence on the right, first uphill, then downhill, and then uphill again and turning slightly to the right to meet the next wood. Here the path initially keeps to the edge of the wood on your left, before leaving it at a corner and heading to a gate into the next wood across the hillside.

Through this gate follow the track, bearing left at the fork a short way in. This will lead you to a crossroads of tracks where you turn right on the grassy track leading downhill. This leads to yet another junction, but you go straight over, still gently downhill. The track bends to the left and then starts to approach another junction of main tracks, but as you approach this you need to keep a sharp eye out. Before you reach this junction, there is a wide grassy track off to the left. Ignore this, but not far beyond it a darker narrower track leads off to the left, again before the junction of main tracks. Turn left down this, but before you've taken a couple of steps, bear right onto the narrower path which leads darkly off between the conifers.

Keep on this down and across the hillside till you come to a junction of different plantings in a lighter more airy spot. Here you head straight down the hillside to a stile into a field. It is at this point, as you walk down the field to the footbridge across the stream, that you can see the abbey remains away to your right. Over the bridge, turn right and go through the gate ahead into the next field. Once in this head to the right of the bungalow at the top of the field and at the old barns. Cross the fence by the barns, your last awkward crossing, and walk round them to the road, turning right on it to return to your vehicle.

LLANDDEWI-YSTRADENNI

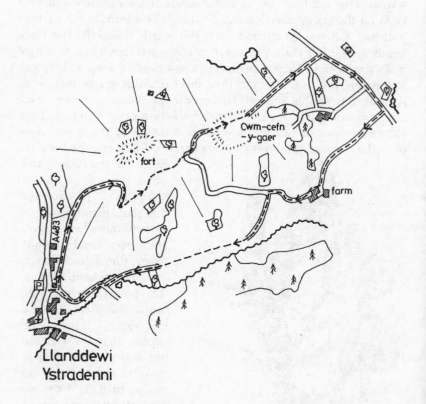

One and a half hours.

A walk largely on tracks with an initial ascent of reasonable scope, with resultant wide views over fields and moorland. In addition one hillfort is passed and an old settlement walked through. Most of the route is in good order, though there is one boggy stretch to cross. As I walked this in a dry spring, it caused me no problem, but if the weather has been wet, then you may need to take greater care.

Park in Llanddewi-Ystradenni, towards the northern end of the road through the village itself.

Walking north along the road there is a large farm on the right, then a field beyond it on the roadside, at the end of which there is a pair of older cottages side on to the road. Just before these is a gate onto a track. Go through this gate, bearing left round the cottages onto a track which follows the gardens of houses on the left. Beyond the houses it keeps on rising up the hillside, passing through a gate onto a steeper section of hillside. The track soon bends to the right up the side of a gully, then bends further right to a small quarry near the top of the slope. The track turns round to the left at this quarry, and then peters out. However, keep walking on the same line you've walked past the quarry along the side of the hill, and passing the hill-fort ramparts away to your left. Towards the end of the field your route drops down slightly to a gate. Go through this, and then follow the old track along the overgrown hedge on your right. You drop downhill into a little hollow, after which the route bends slightly right to another gate.

Through this you enter the boggy patch, where you want to head across to the fence on the right, following this up towards the higher end of the patch. As the bog peters out, walk up the rise to join a gravelled track, on which you turn left. Follow this up and through the ramparts of Cefn-y-gaer. Once in the settlement, keep to the fence on your left, and by following this through the old settlement it will lead you back onto a track. Just keep on this and it, in turn, will lead you to a minor road.

Turn right on the road, and walk downhill till it does a little jink left and right, and where you can see a pool away on your left. Just beyond this a track leads off to the right. Turn onto this and follow it along to the farm ahead. At the edge of the farm the track splits, and you take the right-hand branch to walk round the outside of all the farm buildings and the farmhouse. Beyond the farm the track bends round to the right, crosses a stream and after passing through a gate, splits once more.

Take the left-hand split which follows the valley bottom. Just keep on this track which crosses several fields, through one of which the track is more of a path. After passing some pools on the left, the track jinks right and left, then at the end of the next field, it bends to the right and returns to where the walk started.

SOURCE OF THE LUGG

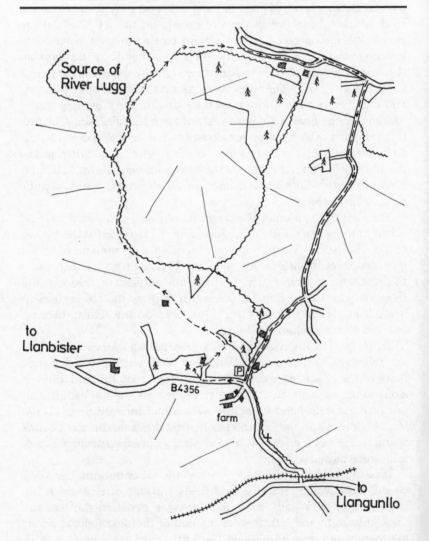

One and a half hours.

A walk across fields, up a rocky gully through which the Lugg flows and then across heather clad moorland, returning via farmland again. The walk is on a mixture of tracks and paths and involves a bit of a scramble by the side of the Lugg at one point.

In Presteigne take the B4356 to Llangunllo and Llanbister, turning right and left over the A488. Once through Llangunllo continue on the B4356 turning sharp right under the railway. The road then bends to the right and left past some houses and on the next major bend left you want to park where you see a track off to the right, and another off to the left leading to a collection of farm buildings.

Walk on up the road for a few hundred yards till you reach a sunken lane on the right with a gate immediately past it which leads onto a stony track curving through a field. Walk up this track, which swings right past some stone buildings on your left. Past these the track bends left again and goes uphill, bending left again once through another gate. At the next gate the track appears to end, but go through the gate into the field and follow the hollow in the ground to the hedge on its far side. Turn right in front of the hedge and follow it up to the gate ahead through which you pass and continue to follow the fence round on your left, passing another stone building in a hollow in the ground on your left. Pass through a further gate into another field and ahead you'll see the Lugg's rocky gully. Turn to the right of this and walk down the field, heading for the middle of the boundary down the hillside—you'll eventually see a gate in the fence. Pass through this onto the moor.

Walk up the Lugg, taking the right-hand stream at all major junctions on each occasion. On the last section the cleft narrows, and depending upon how much water is coming down the Lugg you may need to clamber up out of the cleft and rejoin the stream at the top.

Once out on the open moorland, follow the dip in the ground between the low rises on either side and this will take you in a gentle arc to the right eventually, and fairly suddenly, bringing you to the corner of a wood. Follow this wood along on your right, the paths becoming tracks which pass an old tumbledown lodge. Beyond this you pass through a gate onto a gravelled track. Turn right on this and it will lead you to another corner of the wood. Here turn right (but not sharp right) onto the waymarked Glyndwr's Way, and go through the gate onto a wide track which initially passes between two plantations. This will lead you gently downhill and after about a mile you'll reach a valley bottom. Here there is a crossroads of tracks and you turn right. This track will lead you out to your vehicle.

OFFA'S DYKE ABOVE
LLANFAIR WATERDINE

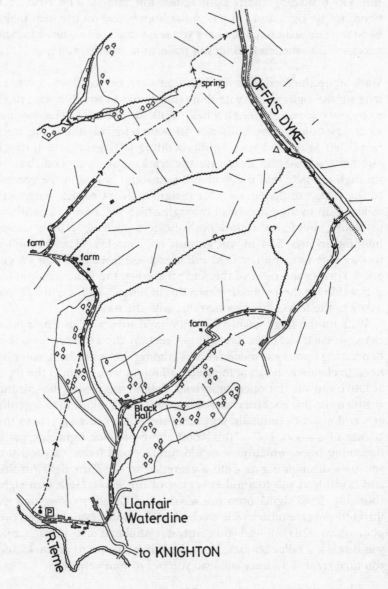

One and three-quarter hours.

A walk in fields, open hillsides, bluebell woods and along part of Offa's Dyke. On a mixture of tracks, paths and lanes. There are ascents to make, but none too steep, and only one slightly awkward fence crossing to make.

You can park at the Red Lion in Llanfair Waterdine if you fancy a drink afterwards—there was real ale when we visited even though no mention was made of it outside. The village can be reached by turning north off the B4355 Newtown to Knighton road in Lloyney, keeping on this minor road till you reach the pub.

From the pub, head west on the road. After you've passed the church on your left, turn through the first gate you come to on the right, to enter the field beyond the church. Follow the boundary on your right up past the church to the top of the field and then briefly along the top boundary till you come to a gate. Go through this and shadow the boundary on your right and you'll quickly meet a track. Turn right on to this. This track will lead you in to the next field and across a corner of it to the one beyond. Here the track ends and you turn slightly to the left—you might be able to make out the slightly level line of the old course of the track—to head for the wood on the far side.

You should join the wood at a point where another track, coming up from the right, enters it. Go across this track and slant down the hillside, where you'll be amongst many bluebells if you've come at the right time of year. You will presently find yourself in the corner of a fenced-off area, and the best place to cross out is in the corner, where we found a makeshift stile of sorts. Continue crossing down the slope on the far side of this fence—you'll pass out of the wood proper and soon afterwards see a stile out onto the lane below. Head for and cross this stile.

Turn left on the lane. This will lead you round the hillside and past a farm and associated buildings on your right. Beyond these it rises up to another set of farm buildings, but as you reach these, you turn sharp right onto a track which slants across the hillside, then turns more directly up it. Further on it turns more to the right once more and, passing through a couple of fields, with a fence always to your right, will eventually lead you out on to the open hillside. Here you turn slightly more to the left, the path keeping to the left of the highest part of the ridge along which you're walking. As you cross over the ridge you'll start to see a gorse covered patch of ground at the head of the cwm on your left, and you aim for this, never descending the hillside. As you approach the gorse, you'll meet another track, on which you turn left.

This track will lead you down the hillside and below a spring. Keep on the track up the hillside on the far side of the spring and as you reach the top of this ridge, turn right through a gate on to a track which leads up towards Offa's Dyke. This track eventually peters out, and when it does so, bear half right and you'll come to a gate in the corner of the field. Pass through the myriad of gates and stiles here to clamber up on to the dyke.

Turn right on the dyke and follow it along, eventually passing a small Dutch barn on the left. Not far beyond this, almost as the dyke meets a small larch wood on the left, you come to a track leading off to the right. Turn right on to this and follow it down as it swings down and round the hillside. As you near a large group of barns, the track crosses a cattle grid. Once over this, turn immediately right through a gate and walk down the hillside to join another track at the valley bottom. Turn right on this and follow it round the hillside to another house, after which it drops downhill back towards the valley bottom, and then bends to the right. Continue on the track which will presently pass through another farmyard and rises slightly to meet a larger lane. Turn left on this and follow it down to the road, turning right on this to return to the Red Lion.

34

A note on Offa's Dyke

Shortly after 700A.D. Mercia, under its ruler Æthalbald, emerged as the most powerful Saxon kingdom south of the Humber. But Æthalbald was murdered and for a while the state was engulfed in civil war, from which Offa eventually emerged as victor, becoming king in 757. By 784 he had restored relatively peaceful conditions, and had enlarged the kingdom at the expense of that of East Anglia.

To delineate his territory, which was centred on his capital at Tamworth, Offa ordered the construction in the west of the dyke bearing his name. This was not designed, like Hadrian's Wall, as a permanently fortified border, but as a raised boundary which could be patrolled along its crest by mounted soldiers. Thus it was planned to largely run along the western crests of the hills to give these troops wide commanding views into the valleys of central Wales. The town of Knighton even derives its name from the old English word cnicht, meaning, originally, a young man and later, a horseman.

The line of the dyke runs for a distance of 149 miles, though the earthwork itself is traceable for just 81 miles. The bank is usually ditched only on the west side, with the spoil from the excavation forming the dyke, though exceptionally there is a ditch on the east side too. In places, even today after centuries of weathering, the dyke reaches six feet in height and sixty feet in breadth.

Though centrally conceived, perhaps by Offa himself, the variations in construction suggest that each neighbouring landowner along the course of the dyke was responsible for the raising of a section. The amount each individual built may have depended upon the area of land he owned or on the number of labourers he had available.

A number of English settlements which appear to pre-date the dyke were placed on the west of the planned route, suggesting that the course of the dyke was at least partially the result of negotiation between Saxon and Welshman, and the Saxons may have relinquished some territory in return for being permitted the most favourable sites for the dyke.

Certainly the two races were by now much intermingled along the border, and Offa's laws provided for a joint English and Welsh board to explain the laws to their respective citizens. These laws included a code for the recovery of stock rustled across the border and another for the safe conduct of either Welshman or Mercian when on the other side of the dyke by a specially appointed guide.

KNUCKLAS

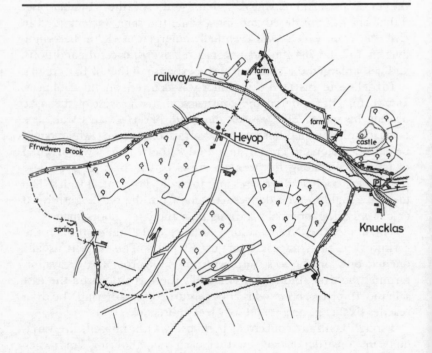

One and a half hours.

A walk in pleasant rolling countryside by and across streams, with no steep ascents. It includes the Victorian Gothic railway viaduct, and the castle mound at Knucklas, and has a very pleasant pub to retire to on completion! It is on a mixture of very minor road, lanes, tracks and paths.

Knucklas lies off the B4355 from Knighton to Beguildy. Coming from Knighton, you cross the railway line, after which you want to take the first left and keep on that road to the centre of the village where you can park.

Walk up the lane to the right of the store in the village, this lane passing along the foot of the castle mound. The castle, and village, derives its name from y Cnwclas meaning the green hillock. The castle appears to have been built in the thirteenth century, undergoing rapid expansion to include several enclosures. At its height there was a masonry wall with four round towers. It is first mentioned in 1246, and subsequently its capture in 1262 when Llewelyn was operating in consort with Simon de Montfort. Soon after this time its use must have lapsed, for it enters no subsequent lists of castles captured in any campaigns, nor was it prepared for defence against Owen Glyndwr, as were so many border castles. Much earlier legend gives the castle mound as the site of the marriage between King Arthur and Guinevere.

The track soon nears the railway line on the left, and passes a quarry on the right, after which it bends uphill to the right. Keep straight on when the main track bends left to a farm, but after not many yards you turn left through a gate into a field near an old shed. Walk along the hedge on your left to the end of the field, where you join a more well marked track. This leads on up the hillside and then along a narrow ridge before dropping down slightly to join another track in front of a farm. Turn left on this track, following it down the hillside till it enters the grounds of another house. Here you turn left through the gate immediately before the house into a field, dropping straight down the hillside to the stiles over the railway line. Take care—the line is still in use.

Over the railway line head slightly to the left of the church, crossing a stream with its bridge in the valley bottom, and then a stile into a builder's yard and out of the yard onto the road via a kissing gate, which has been made for thin people.

On the road beyond, turn right, and walk along this round the bend ahead, and then along the foot of the wood on your left. At the end of this wood, turn left off the road onto a track, itself just to the left of a bungalow. Walk along this track, taking the right-hand fork ahead to keep to the field boundaries on your right. Eventually you will pass through a gate into a large field-cum-rough piece of ground immediately above Dolfelin Farm on your right. Through this patch of ground flows a small stream, emerging from the hillside in a deeply sunk gully on the left. Just before this gully you will see a gate in the fence above you which leads onto a sunken track. Take the track to the left which leads up to this gate, and through it walk up the track to the gate to the next field.

Through this next gate, keep to the top of the bank on the right of the field and so continue to shadow the stream. Presently you'll come to another gate, and go through this to follow the hedge on your left till it makes a right-angled turn away from you. Now head half right to the gate on the far side of the field, passing just above the springs which feed the stream. Through this next gate, follow the hedge on your right, curving around the field till you reach a gate out of it immediately before you reach the farm buildings near the top of the hill.

Once through the gate, turn right and take the left-hand fork in the track. This will lead you to a gate in the corner of the field, through which you pass. Not much further on you reach the corner of the field on your left, and slightly beyond this you want to turn left and shadow the gully on your left downhill. As you near the stream in the valley bottom, you'll pick up a track which leads down and across it, and then up to a gate out onto a road. Go straight across this road to another gate, and once through, bear half left to follow the fence on your left to another gate ahead. Go through this when you reach it and continue to walk on the same line—you can make out the course of an old track leading through this field. This will fairly abruptly lead you over the crest of a narrow ridge, and continue on the same line down to an old gate at the left-hand corner of a farmyard. Go through or over this and out of the yard onto the lanes beyond. Take the right-hand metalled lane downhill, still keeping to much the same direction, and follow this all the way back into Knucklas.

As you approach the village you have further views of the viaduct with the castle site behind. When you reach the road at the end of the lane, turn right to return to your vehicle. Turn right just before the stream to find the pub, the Castle Inn.

CAER CARADOC

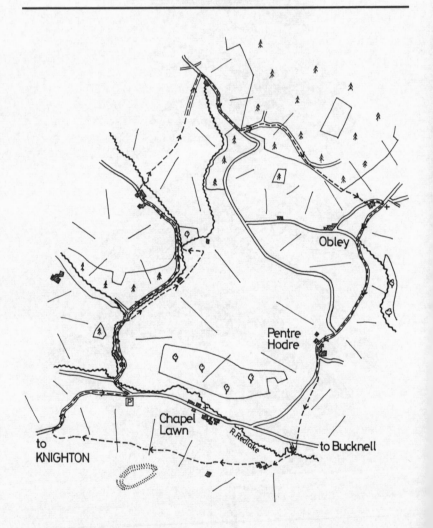

Two and three-quarter hours.

A fair amount of this walk is on very minor road, but which appears to carry only the occasional vehicle. The rest is on tracks and paths and the walk has sweeping views of the hilly countryside of the area.

Caer Caradoc's ramparts are passed, and the hillfort itself is seen from a variety of angles and distances, perched beret-like on the end of its hill. There are several steepish descents, but, somewhat amazingly, only one steepish ascent en route.

Caer Caradoc is one of many hillforts in the neighbourhood which some historian or another has claimed as the site of Caractacus' last stand against the Romans. King of the Catuvellauni, he organised the widespread resistance to the invasion of 43A.D. Defeated in the south, he moved to the territory of the Silures and Dobunni whither the Romans pursued him. Eventually his new alliance was defeated somewhere on the Welsh border, and he fled north to seek shelter with Queen Cartimandua. She, however, betrayed him to the Romans.

From Knighton take the A488 signposted to Clun. Keep on this road till some three miles out from the town, when you turn right near the brow of the road, signposted to Chapel Lawn and Bucknell. Keep on this road till you come to a T-junction with another, which is where you want to park.

When setting off walking, you turn left at this junction as you approached it by vehicle. Round the corner you come to another split in the road, and you bear right. Keep on this road till you come to a bridge over the stream, where you have a choice of routes. You can either keep to the road, where the going is flatter, or make a more interesting diversion, though it does involve passing through one farmyard.

If making the diversion, turn right up the track just before this bridge. This will lead you above the stream to a small farm, which you pass through, leaving its yard via the gate at the far end. Here the track makes a slight detour from the definitive route, and it appears best to keep to the well worn track. Follow this along, it roughly keeping to the contours of the hillside, till it enters a field. Here you bear up the hill to the far right-hand corner of the field, where you leave it via another gate, turning left on to a track. This will lead down past a cottage and over a stream, to rejoin the road, on which you turn right.

If not making the diversion, keep to the road and when you come to a cottage on the right, in front of which a track slants off to the right downhill, the two routes have rejoined.

Carry on along the road and you will soon come to a collection of buildings to left and right, those on the right called Hobarris. Immediately beyond these turn right on the track which goes downhill and crosses the stream. Over the stream keep to the left-hand split in the track, and when this turns to the right, go through the gate ahead on the bend in the track. (Hobarris should be right behind you—if you start to find it on your right, you've gone too far on the track.) In the field, head for the gate to the right of the railway carriage near the skyline. Through this gate you're once more on a track which leads past a clump of Scotch Pines marking the site of a cairn off to the left. Keep on this track to the road ahead, on which you turn right.

Follow this road and you'll come to some forestry plantations, initially on the right, and then on the left as well. Here we make a slight diversion for a while from the definitive path, as that route is blocked by plantings. As you reach the plantation on the left, turn left up the wide forestry track. Keep on this till it bends to the left, when you turn right onto a slightly smaller track. Further on it meets another track, on which you turn right. This will lead you along the edge of the plantation for a short while, but once the track bends left back into the forestry, you need to cross to the fence at the boundary of the plantation on your right. Here you will find a narrow path bang up against the fence—but don't worry, it's quite passable and will lead to stiles! Keep to this path which leads you steeply down the hillside to the corner of the wood. Cross out by the stile here, and follow the fence on your right down the hillside on much the same line. This will lead to another stile in the corner of the field, which you cross, immediately crossing the gate on your right. Then follow the fence on your left down to the gate onto the road.

Turn left on the road and then right at the junction in front of the chapel. Keep to this road, bearing left at the next junction. This will then lead you slightly uphill before following the contours of the hill and turning slightly to the right. As you start to approach another group of buildings, another road leads off to the right, but ignore this and carry straight on. The road bends through a series of farm buildings and then splits. You keep to the right, following the road to Chapel Lawn. However, quite soon after this junction you come to a house on your left, immediately beyond which two gates are set back from the road. Take the left-hand of these and at the gate not many yards in front of it, turn right to follow the hedgerow on your left. Keep following this, almost shadowing the road on your 'right, to the far left-hand corner of the field, where you'll find a stile tucked away. Cross this, and walk down the field towards the buildings in the valley bottom, crossing the stile on the indented corner of the fence which you come to. Then follow the hedge on your left down to the road.

Cross the road and go over the stile on the far side. This next short section of route may be fairly obstructed, in which case pass out to the right and walk down to the farm below. The path now goes through the farmyard, round the rear of the house, through a gate and then across a stream by a bridge. Cross to the stile on the far right-hand corner of the field across the stream. Cross this and head across the next field on the same line. As you walk through the field you'll see the next farm ahead. Aim for the near barn and when you reach it bear right, around it, passing through a gate in the field beyond onto the track which leads to the barns.

Turn right on the track, and at the fork ahead, bear left. As this track curves left to another another farm you turn right through a gate to walk directly up the hillside, passing through a narrow rough patch of ground between two fields. At the end of this you have to cross a fence. Then you follow the broad track up across the hillside on which Caer Caradoc sits. This track swings to the left further on and then comes to a gate into a larger field. Here you are at the closest you'll be to the ramparts. Through this gate, the path keeps to the fence on your right and at the next gate once more becomes a track. Keep to this and it will lead you to a road. Turn right on the road to return to your vehicle.

NORTON

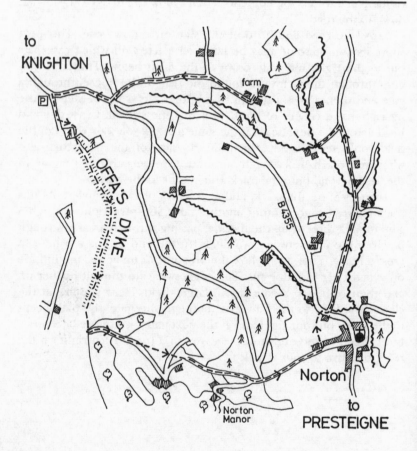

One and a half hours.

This walk includes a reasonably well preserved part of Offa's Dyke with its views over central Wales, as well as tracks through and on the edge of woodland, some of it old oak, some coniferous.

From Presteigne take the B4356 west, and just past the end of the town turn right on to the B4355 to Knighton. After passing through the village of Norton the road starts a long climb uphill. When you reach the top of the hill, park when you come to a lay-by on the left near Offa's Dyke path signs.

Cross the stile on the left and walk across to the track to the left of the gorse strip. Follow the oak waymarking signs of Offa's Dyke path round to the left of the first wood and between it and the second. This leads you on to Offa's Dyke itself which you then follow.

The dyke runs along and then descends the hillside and where it peters out, Offa's Dyke path is signposted to the right. Ignore this and carry on, turning slightly left to reach the gate into the woodland on the left about 200 yards ahead. Pass through this gateway and walk down the track. Pass a narrow conifer plantation on your left and through another gateway you come to an area of open ground above some farm buildings and cottages. Turn left and walk down to the left of the left-hand most cottage, passing through a further gateway on to a metalled lane. Follow this lane round, which overlooks Norton Manor. Further on it bends to the left and then right to descend towards the village of Norton, aiming almost at the church.

Past the first house you come to on the left, turn left up the short track and go through a gate into a field. Cross this field to the gate opposite on the far side, and then bear slightly more to the right in the second field, to pass round a clump of trees and bushes to find another short track which leads down to a gate on to the road. Turn right on the road and almost immediately left on to a metalled lane.

Walk up this lane, bearing left at the split once over a stream, and start to ascend the hillside. Further on a more minor lane leads off downhill to the left, and you take this. In the dip at the bottom, you cross a stream and have to enter what appears to be someone's driveway in order to cross a little bridge on the right and pass through a gate beyond onto the line of an old sunken track. Walk along this, soon to aim almost at the farm which appears perched near the top of the rise. Pass through a gate into the next field, and continue on the track up to a gate into the farmyard.

The way onto the public path from here is not clear, so turn left through the farmyard and walk down the farm's access road which will lead you back to the B road. Turn right on this to return to your vehicle.

PILLETH

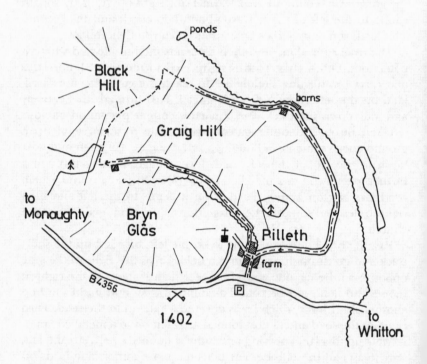

One and a quarter hours.

A circuit of a grassy hill above the battlefield of Pilleth, with views across the border country, along well maintained tracks and gentle slopes. (You can visit the church to see the pieces of armour and weaponry from the Battle of Pilleth. This was fought on 22 June 1401 when Edmund Mortimer was taken prisoner, and Sir Walter Devereux of Weobley and Sir Robert Whitney, Knight Marshall to the king, were killed in a battle against the Welsh forces of Glyndwr. The clump of trees on the hillside above the church marks the burial place of those killed. Henry IV refused to pay the ransom demanded for Edmund Mortimer after the battle, so the latter joined forces with Glyndwr.)

From Presteigne take the B4356 west to Llanbister and Newtown. About three miles west from Presteigne you pass over a crossroads with the B4357 at Whitton and about three-quarters of a mile further on you come to Pilleth, recognizable by the church up on a hillside on the right. Park near the lane at the foot of the hill on which the church nestles.

Walk up the lane to the farmyard and turn towards the church. (The path to the church goes on ahead through a small gate.) The track then turns round to the right and passes through a gate as it turns left once more. The track crosses a stream and then climbs gently up the hillside. It eventually heads towards the lower, left-hand end of a wood on the hillside ahead, below which you come to a gate into a field. Pass through this gate and turn right to take the path along the hedge and into the edge of the wood. Keep the wood on your left and walk steeply uphill.

At the far end of the wood go through another gate and onto the hillside. The track initially follows some fencing on your right, but passing through one gate, it then follows a hedge and fencing on your left. When the ponds in the valley floor are visible the track turns right immediately after passing through another gate. It then follows the valley on the near side of the fence, one field up from the ponds. When you reach some farm buildings, the path actually passes them to their right—go through the gate into the field just above the buildings. Keep the buildings on your immediate left and when you've turned the far corner you'll see a stile on which to cross out back on to the track. This now has a metalled surface and will lead you back round the hillside to the farm you started from.

NEW RADNOR

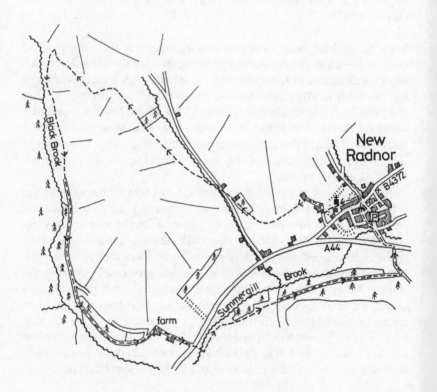

Two and a half hours.

Largely on tracks in valley bottoms in Radnor Forest, but including an ascent across one ridge. Wide ranging views from the crest of the ridge, which is reached after a not too severe climb. Includes open hillside, and fields in the lower valleys. Passes by and through some woodland, and there is one awkward stile to cross.

Park in New Radnor near the pubs to the south of the castle mound—either of which makes a convenient watering-hole on the walk's completion.

Walk up the road towards the castle mound, turning right at the T-junction. After just a few yards take the signposted path to the left which leads to the edge of the castle mound itself. Keep to the fence on your left and the path will lead you into the churchyard. Continue through the churchyard, leaving it to the right of the house below the church to turn immediately right and enter the field to the west of the church via the little gate.

Turn right through this gate and go through the gate ahead into the next field. Then turn half left and head towards the building on the far side of the field, leaving the field by another small gate. Here you will find yourself on a lane on which you turn right. Walk up the lane which presently bends to the left before reducing in width to a path which leads between two hedges. At the end of this path you come to a gate into a field. Carry on through the field on the same line, the path then gradually swinging to the right before leaving it via another gate. Here you emerge onto a track which leads down across open hillside towards the valley bottom. As you reach this you pass a wood on your right and pick up a metalled lane along which you walk, till you come to a footpath signposted off to the left just before a gate into the Radnor Forest danger area.

This path slants up across the far hillside, before turning left and right to pass some old quarries and emerge onto the top of the ridge. As it nears the summit the path splits and you take the left-hand one across the ridge and down the far side, presently to join a major track, which swings round to the left and leads you down the valley back towards the main road. You soon cross a gate into a field above the stream and opposite a conifer plantation. Walk through this field to join a track at the far side, which then follows the edge of the woodland on your right.

The track splits further on, and you take the right-hand fork which leads you between two clumps of woodland. This track soon bends to the left to follow the left-hand clump, and swings you round towards the Vron farm. The track passes immediately above the farm and enters the farmyard at the end of the buildings. Leave the yard by the farm's drive and walk down to the main road.

Cross straight over the road and enter the field beyond by the gate. Bear marginally left across the field to cross the stream by the bridge provided. Then turn left and follow the stream to the gate at the far end of the field. Go through the gate and bear half-right to another gate at the top of this small field. This will lead you onto a path which in turn will lead you into a clearing in the woodland.

Here the path becomes indistinct, and you want to head for the far left-hand corner of the clearing, in other words dropping downhill only slightly as you cross this wide patch of ground. At the end of this clearing there is the awkward stile to cross, and then a bank to clamber up to join a forestry road in the conifer plantation. Walk along this road till you join a metalled track on which you turn left to walk back down to the main road.

Turn left and almost immediately right on the road to return to New Radnor.

A note on New Radnor

Harold Godwinson is often reputed to have founded the town and castle in 1064 as a stronghold to defend the route from central Wales into England. He certainly advanced as far as this in his pursuit of the Welsh after their sacking of Hereford, but it is not definitely known that he founded the town.

After the Conquest the territory was in the possession of Philip de Breos, who almost certainly built a castle, laid out the gridiron street pattern for the borough and constructed the earthen town bank around the settlement.

The castle remained with the de Breos family until around 1240 when it passed by marriage to the Mortimers, but before then it had been captured five times—in 1163 and 1195 by Rhys ap Gruffyd, when he also defeated a relieving army led by Mortimer and de Saye; in 1213 by Llewelyn; in 1216 by King John and in 1231 by Llewelyn again. It is quite possible that Henry III recaptured it during his stay at Painscastle. Certainly Henry's brother, Richard Earl of Cornwall and King of the Romans, repaired it in 1231 and the Mortimers subsequently rebuilt it. However in 1264 it was once again taken by the Welsh when allied to Simon de Montfort. These Welsh advances were lost when Edward I invaded Wales.

In 1401 it once more passed into Welsh hands, this time those of Glyndwr who beheaded the garrison of sixty. By 1405 Henry IV had retaken possession and he installed a force of 30 men at arms and 150 archers under Richard, Lord de Grey. Almost 250 years later the town was held for Charles I, but was captured after a short siege.

A part of the curtain wall was still standing around 1850, and various excavations have unearthed cannon balls, cannon, floors, foundations and a well, but now only the substantial earthworks can be seen, dominating the town.

At the southern end of the main street stands a white marble profile, in Victorian Gothic, of Sir George Cornewall Lewis, New Radnor's M.P. from 1855 to 1863 and who was Chancellor of the Exchequer, Home Secretary and War Minister in different administrations under Palmerston.

LLANDEGELY ROCKS

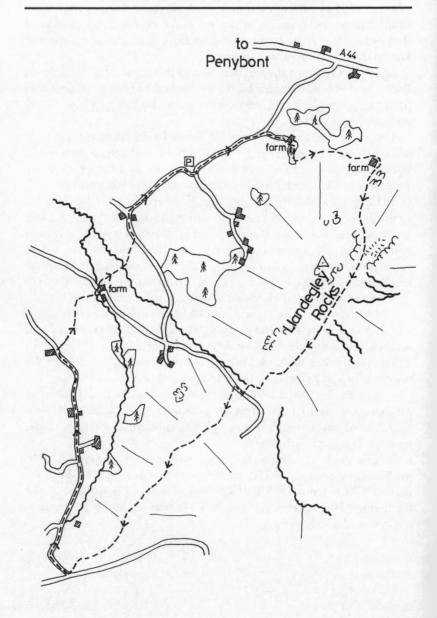

to Penybont

A44

farm

P

farm

farm

Llandegely Rocks

Two hours.

A walk largely on paths, some very minor road and even less tracks. It involves a circuit of Llandegley Rocks, with a couple of short, and on one occasion sharp, ascents. A short section of the walk diverges from the definitive footpath route to reduce the number of obstructions. There is also one stream and fence to cross, though this can be avoided with a longer diversion. The are wide all round views to Radnor Forest, south towards and beyond Builth and over Llandrindod. There are old quarries and small rocky pools.

From Llandegely on the A44 Rhayder to Kington road, head west towards Rhyader. About a quarter of a mile out of the village, take the first and unsignposted road off to the left. Drive down this, passing a farm lane off to the left, till you reach a metalled lane off to the left. The best place to park is on the verge beyond this junction.

Walk back down the road to that first farm lane, and turn right up it. Your route follows this through the farmyard ahead and out through a gate onto the hillside. Keep to the track beyond the gate, this bends right, and then take the first branch left which leads to an old quarry. Your route bears left in front of the quarry, and as you walk along the steep bank here, you will near a corner of fencing. The path slopes up across the hillside from this point, slightly diverging from the line of the fencing which you leave to your left. Further on the path crosses a small gully to a gate, through which you keep to the fencing on your left.

This will soon lead you right, then left, then right again past the remains of some field boundaries for a small farm set back into the rocks on your right. Here you will meet a stoned track leading right and up the hillside, passing by this farmhouse. Take this track, and it leads you out onto the hillside, heading straight for Llandegley Rocks and keeping a field to your left. At the end of this field, the track meets another on which you turn left to pass betwen the rocks and a hill on the left which is the site of an early settlement. When you meet a fence between the two hills, go through the gate and turn right, so that you have a fence between you and the heights of Llandegley Rocks. Very soon you'll come to a gate into a feld, and you cross the next fields on the same line, shadowing the rocks.

After a few fields, you start to appear above a flatter area where the next section of the ridge of Llandegley Rocks is set back further to the west. This is where we briefly leave the definitive footpath. Turn slightly to the right to initially head for the outcrop of rocks on this next section of hill. As you approach it, you'll see a track passing below these outcrops, and on your side of the hillside a junction of fences. Head to this junction, crossing over into the field on the right. Walk down the fence on your left to the gate and out onto the track at the bottom of the field. Turn right on the track, pass through the gate across it, and then turn left to follow the fence on your left up the hill. (When you become adjacent to the first field boundary on your left, you're back on the definitive footpath.)

Keep to this fence all the way along, only diverging from it when you're right above the track which has been gradually nearing the line of fence from the left. Cross a corner of the enclosure and above a small quarry, to pass through the gate by which the track enters onto the hillside. As you approach this gate keep an eye out for the old grassy track which rises up the next section of the hill, for this is the route you want to take.

Walk up this track, passing some grassy ridges on your left, and a few larch trees further on on your right. As it nears the crest of the hill the track jinks right and then left to leave the summit to your left. Continue on this track which will lead you to a gate onto a road.

Turn right on the road, the road soon bending to the right. Keep to this road for a fair while, passing a new bungalow on the right and then a house on the left. Round a bend beyond that, the road does a little right and left past another farm. Here you turn right through a gate and walk across the field to the gate on the far side. Through this follow the hedge on your left to the end of this next field, where you will join a track. Turn right on this and follow it down to the road, crossing onto it via a ford.

If you want to avoid what could prove an awkward stream and fence crossing, but which involves a longer walk, turn right on the road and keep to it to return to your vehicle.

Otherwise, turn left on the road, and immediately past the farmhouse walk up to the right-hand of two little gates, passing through this to the gate immediately above it. Through this next gate, follow the hedge on your right to the stream ahead. Here you have to cross it and the fence beyond by the best means available. Once over cross to the corner of hedge opposite, following the hedge on your right till you come to a gate. Go through this, then follow the same hedge, now on your left to the gate in the corner of the field. Go through this, and turn left on the road to return to your vehicle.

GARREG DDU RESERVOIR

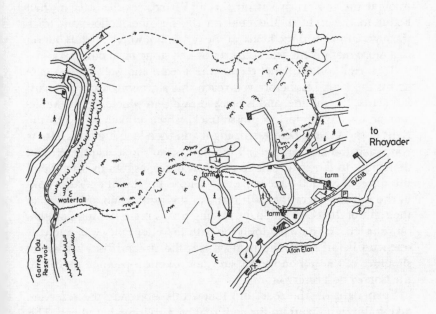

Two hours.

A walk past cascading streams and Elan valley reservoirs with extensive views, and on paths and tracks in generally good condition. However it is worth ensuring wearing waterproof footwear as there are some boggy patches on the hilltops, and after rain many of the paths can become small streams.

From Rhayader take the B4518 Elan Valley road. Out of the town go past one turning off to the right, then over a small crossroads. Go past one farm set at the foot of the hillside on the right, and then park near the entrance track to a white painted farm on the right which nestles by some woodland. If you reach a double bend sign on the road, then you've gone just too far.

Walk on down the road towards the double bend sign, and bear half right through the gate onto the track on the right. This leads to a farm, by the side of which you bear right on the track by the side of the stream, this passing under a bridge further ahead. Yet further on the track ends at a junction in the stream, but you cross the stream on your right and walk up the steep bank ahead, joining another track at the top. Turn left on this and it crosses the stream, then bends to the right in the field on the far side. Follow this track through a total of three fields, at the far end of which it leads out on to a more major lane near some renovated stone farm buildings.

Turn right on this lane, recross the stream and walk up to a gate across the lane. Just before you reach this a grassy track leads sharp left across the hillside, and is marked by a sign which says 'no vehicular access'. Walk up this grassy track, which initially keeps to the right of the stream, before crossing it and then keeping to its left. As you reach the crest of the hill the path swings first slightly left and then right to cross a dip between rocky outcrops. On the far side of this dip it bends left once more and follows the dip into a large bowl in the hillside. Here the path turns to the right again and keeps to the right of the bowl, gradually picking up a stream flowing downhill on your left. As you walk down the path the Elan valley will gradually open up before you. The path crosses the stream, rises across the shoulder of the hill on the far side, and then drops quite sharply to the Garreg ddu reservoir.

Turn right on the road and follow this alongside the reservoir, taking the right-hand no through road at a split further ahead. This will lead you gradually up the hillside, and keep a look out through the trees to your left for you will eventually see the dam to the Pen-y-garreg reservoir further up the valley. This can be an impressive sight if the water is streaming over it. Keep to the right-hand track further ahead, and then turn right in front of the gateway to a house, to shadow the wood on your left. Where the wood bends away to the left a few hundred yards ahead, you want to take the path which clambers quite steeply up the hillside.

Fairly soon however this turns more to the left to shadow the wood and soon meets another track at a hairpin bend. Turn right onto this track, and it will lead you up the hillside. As you near the top you have a boggy patch of ground to cross on much the same line as you've just been walking, but where the track can be slightly indistinct. But on the far side you will rediscover the track, which turns slightly more to the right. Keep on this well formed track on

which you will start to make a gradual descent. You cross a couple of boggy patches and then a stream which flows out from the hillside on the right. Beyond this keep to the left-hand track at the various splits it makes, and it will bring you back to the stream further on. Here keep to the right of the stream, ignoring the track which crosses it, and you will gradually swing round the hillside to your right in a gentle arc. As you descend you will pass a cottage on your left and then come to a corner of a wood. Keep to the right of the wood and soon you will be passing by old deciduous wood-land and above another cottage to your left. The track will eventually meet a metalled lane, which you cross and go through a gate onto a track between two hedgerows, a track which takes your route half left. Go down this and you will come to a farm-yard. Go through the gateway into the farmyard, leaving it via the left-hand of two gateways to the right of the house. This will lead you back to the B4518 and your vehicle.

LLANAFAN-FAWR

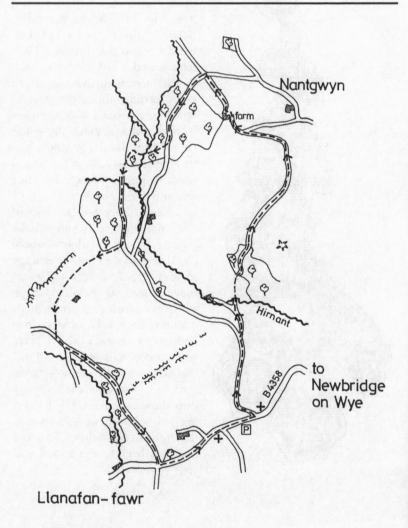

Nantgwyn

farm

Hirnant

to
Newbridge
on Wye

B4358

Llanafan-fawr

One and a half hours.

A walk in fairly open hill country and the fields on the lower slopes, with wide all round views except to the north. A small section of forestry is involved, with an awkward fence crossing, otherwise the walk is on lanes, tracks and a short section of B road, though even this has generally wide verges enabling you to keep off the road. Some short but sharpish ascents.

Take the A483 from Builth to Llandovery. On the edge of Builth you cross the River Irfon, immediately after which take the minor road to the right, passing the golf course. Keep on this road, which eventually crosses a cattle grid onto some open hill land. Keep left at the road junction here to Llanafan-fawr, and when you reach a T-junction with the B road just in front of the hills, you want to park on the verge on your right. (Alternatively take the B4358 from Newbridge on Wye to Beulah and Llandovery. Park on the verge just before the second minor road left, this road signposted Builth five and a half miles. If you reach a chapel round the bend on a narrow piece of road, you've gone just too far.)

Walk up the B road towards Newbridge, taking the lane off to the left just before the house and church on the crest of the hill. Follow this lane as it bends round to the right, and where it bends left to shadow a stream in the valley ahead, go through the gate on the right onto a track. Follow this down and round to the left where you start to approach a farm. But not far round this bend, turn through the gate on the right which leads down an old track to ford the stream. Presently you'll reach the end of this track, with gates to left and right. Take the left-hand, to then follow the stream on your right (in other words keeping to much the same line as you've just been walking) and at the end of the field you're in you'll once more join a main track.

You now stay on this track for some considerable time. It makes a fairly sharp ascent through old woodland and out onto the hillside, before turning slightly to the right. Just keep on it, and round the hillside, it starts to bend to the left. It's on this stretch that you'll have the widest views. Round the hillside the track drops down towards a farm, and you follow the track into the farmyard, turning left beyond the buildings to head towards the farm house, but then leaving the yard by the continuation of the lane to the right of the farmhouse. This almost immediately turns sharp right and soon left again to rise up over a small hill and then drop sharply down into the next valley bottom. Through a gate at the start of a flat piece of ground you come to a crossroads of tracks, and here you turn left to pass a small quarry and go through a gate into some woodland.

Keep on the track through the woodland, till you come to a barn on the left. Here keep on what is now a less well used track straight ahead and downhill till you come to a line of telegraph poles. Here it is best to turn right (the true course of the definitive path has been obscured by the plantings) and follow the swathe made for these poles, dropping steeply down to cross a stream, and then rising gently to a fence at the far end of the wood. Here is the awkward crossing, but once over, turn left on the track, passing almost immediately through a gate and then following the track. (If you want to shorten the walk, just keep to this—you'll meet your old route eventually.)

To keep to the full walk, take the grassy track off to the right immediately at the end of the woodland on your right. After another sharpish ascent this will lead you out onto a saddle on the hillside, where the track abruptly ends. However, other tracks have made their appearance to your right and if you cross to join these, you'll soon pick up the large track which takes the left-hand side of a gully running down the far side of the hill. This will lead you down to a lane, on which you turn left to return to the B road. Turn left when you reach this to return to your vehicle.

BEULAH

Two and a half hours.

A walk on a mixture of minor road, tracks and paths by streams, through woodland, both forestry and old oak, past rocky outcrops and crags and with a range of wide views. Much of the walk is on gentle slopes, but there are two short but quite steep ascents. There are also several largish streams to ford, or log bridges to cross. (The walk can be reduced in length, though so also reducing the views and variety of scenery, by keeping to the minor road till the chapel is reached.)

From Beulah head west to Llandovery on the A483, turning right on the minor road at the edge of the village, signposted to Abergwesyn. Bear left at the junction with the church on your right, and soon the road swings left to cross a stream in a flattish valley, and you can park on the corner beyond this crossing.

Carry on walking along the road, opposite the large house called Llwyn Madoc. You pass a pool between you and the house and then come adjacent to the walled garden to the west of the house. Almost opposite the end of this, a track leads off almost back on you to the left, and you take this rocky route. It passes through a gate and out into a field, where you turn right, keeping to the sunken route. This swings round an almost demolished old cottage, then bears right towards a couple of barns. Turn right just in front of these. This sunken track will quickly lead you to a gate into a field, where you keep to the fence on the right, this staying just to the right of the high ground along this ridge. You pass through the very old remains of one fence, and then another gate after which you emerge onto a much more definite track once more, this shadowing the old oak woodland below to your right.

Keep to this track, and it leads round the craggy hills on your left, before dropping to pass through some gates into a sheep handling area on the corner with some forestry plantation. As you approach this, keep an eye out for a gravelled track which makes an abrupt start on the hillside to the right of this forestry— for you will eventually head for this. But first the path passes through the handling area, then keeps to the boundary of the wood on your left for some 300 to 400 yards. After this distance, turn at right angles to the right and walk across the field till you join the gravelled track referred to.

Now turn onto this and walk round the hillside in a gentle arc, passing round the streams which flow from the hillside, and then heading back on yourself and gently descending the hillside. Further on the track makes a sharp right turn and then passes through a farmyard and via a ford or bouncy bridge to the minor road.

Turn left on this, and walk along it till you come to the chapel on your right. Go past this, and clamber up the bank beyond to join a track on which you turn right and which leads along the back of the chapel. Keep to this, passing the chapel once more, and as the track starts to bend to the right, take the track to the left and sharply uphill. Further on this zig-zags up the hillside, and then meets a wider forestry road. Go straight over this, and take the track going down the other side. As it starts to level out, you meet a track leading sharply off to the right. Take this, which leads through the woodland, eventually coming to a gate at the far end.

Keep to the track which heads towards the stream, and then turns right and continues to drop down to meet it. Here you can either ford the stream, or keep to the bank for few more yards and cross the log bridge. Once over join the metalled lane ahead, and keep to this for a while, passing above a meander and until the road comes very close to the stream, when it veers off to the left. Here take the right-hand of the gates ahead, and follow the track, again crossing the stream by the ford or footbridge and up the far side, where the track turns to the left. (This last short section is not shown as a definitive footpath, but because an alternative route is obstructed by fences, I've incorporated this short section as the easiest way of avoiding these obstructions.)

Keep to the track, it passing a barn and cottage on the left, then further on makes a sharp turn to the right. Keep to this until you've passed a wood off to the left. Here you meet a track from the right, and the definitive path leads off through a gate on the left straight over a field to the farm on the far side. Once over this field pass through a gate in front of the farm and keep to the track on the far side, to then walk away from the farmhouse and down the farm's driveway to the road. Turn right on the road to return to your vehicle.

BUILTH WELLS

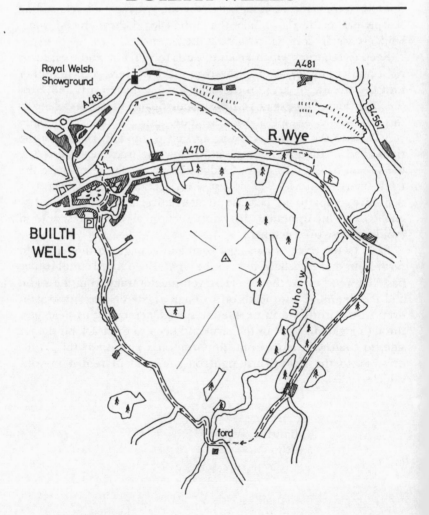

One and a half hours.

This walk includes a section of the River Wye, some of Builth itself and gentle valleys to the town's west. It is generally on good tracks, though there is also a four hundred yard or so length of main road to walk along.

Park in Builth and walk out of the town on the A470 Abergavenny/ Brecon road. Just past the garage on your right near the edge of town, turn down the farmyard entrance on the left, following the tarmac and concrete that winds through the buildings and leads down to the Wye. Go through the gate at the end of the concrete

Wye.
banks of the
o cross—one
e but barbed
k and in the
s a gate-cum-
d woodland.
ly ahead was
ce. Carry on
ood stile out
the fence at
he gate onto

The definitive footpath at the beginning of this walk is currently being restored and you should not walk through the farmyard mentioned in the first paragraph on p65. Instead, on a bend to the right on the A470 before you reach the garage referred to, take the lane to the left. Immediately across the stream turn left down the path on the stream's bank. Cross the stile at the end, and turn right to soon join the track which runs parallel with the river. Then continue as per the second paragraph, keeping close to the Wye.

Turn left down the main road, cross the stream and opposite a farm on the left, turn right up a little metalled drive with a letterbox on its corner. This leads up a valley to a farm and you enter its farmyard. At the yard's far end two gates lead out of it. Take the right-hand one into the field beyond and the track follows the edge of the wood on your left and leads along to a gate into the next field. Through this turn slightly right to the opening opposite into the further field, and once in this field bear downhill to the far right-hand corner where you'll pick up a track which leads down to a gate. This is overgrown and easier to climb over, but once across, follow the hedge on your right and you'll soon join a better path which leads to the house ahead. Immediately in front of this house the path turns right between the house's boundary fence and a hedge and will lead you to a choice of ford or bridge over the river ahead.

The track now gains a metalled surface and zig-zags up the hillside before dividing. Take the right-hand fork and this will lead you gently back to Builth. When you meet the major junction in front of the old castle mound, if you bear right and look out for a stile on your left you can clamber up the old mound and its two ditches.

RHULEN & CREGRINA

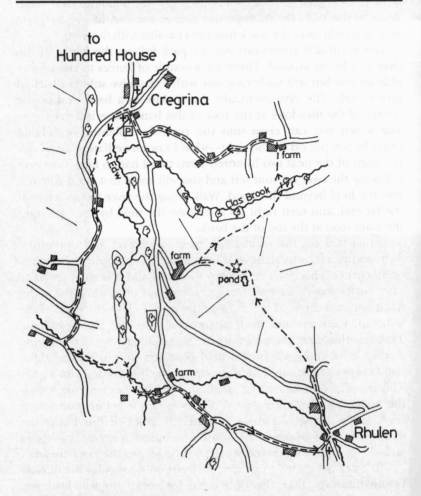

One and three-quarter hours.

A walk along flanks of the valley hills, though there are a few steep
ascents and descents involved. On a mixture of very minor roads,
tracks and paths across fields. There are three awkward fence crossings where no stiles are provided, but at the time I walked it, these
were fairly easily crossed thanks to well positioned bracing posts, lack

of barbed wire, or even rotten fence posts! The two simple but interesting churches at Cregrina and Rhulen can both be visited, and the Edw and other streams are crossed and recrossed.

Park in Cregrina near the bridge over the River Edw.

Walk up the road past Cregrina Church. The church is comparatively plain and simple, but with a fairly roughly carved rood screen. Past the church, turn left through the gate into the field. Don't follow the track down to the river's edge, but walk above the steep drop, curving through the field to the far right-hand corner. Here is one of the less easy fence crossings back out onto the road. Turn left on the road and continue walking along it a reasonable distance.

You eventually come to a junction on a sharp bend to the left where a minor road leads right signposted to Latho. Continue left on the main road. Not far beyond this the road drops steeply down to another sharp bend left, with another lane off to the right. Again bear left on the road, but this time, before the road crosses the stream round the bend, bear left through a gate. This will lead you onto an old broad track on a bank above the stream. Follow this, slightly overgrown in places, and it will lead you out through a gate into a wide field. Here, leave the main track which keeps ahead, and turn right and follow the hedge on your right, turning further right when it peters out and head to the bottom far corner of the field. Here you cross a stile and a stream and then follow the river bank till you come to a metal bridge across the Edw. Go across this, and then head to the left of the farm ahead. This will bring you to a gate into the farmyard. Walk through the gateway, bearing left in the farmyard and walk down its drive to the road ahead.

Turn right on the road, and left at the two junctions in quick succession after the chapel. This road will bring you to Rhulen Church, which again is worth a visit. It is even more plain than that of Cregrina. Both Rhulen and Cregrina probably acted as small outposts of the early monastery based at Glascwm, and Rhulen is built in a simple early Norman style. The large porch was used for parish meetings, whilst inside the interior is dim as it is lit by only two windows. The west wall has a noticeable lean, though it seems to have been quite stable for several centuries.

Carry on down the road past the church, crossing the brook, and then gently ascending the hillside to a T-junction with a no through road to the right. Here cross the T to the gate ahead, and walk up the stoned track. When this bends right, continue on to the corner of the field, to another of the awkward fence crossings. You can cross a stile on your left, but then you need to cross the fence on your right so that you are in the highest field of the three that meet in this corner. The path now clings to the side of the hill, crossing this field to a point just above an old quarry on the far side, this being marked by a series of bumps and hollows. Go through the gate above the quarry into the next field, and keep gently ascending the hillside. As you cross this you will see a pond ringed by fencing, to the right of some aeriels. Take the gate on the right at the far end of the pond, and turning left onto a stony track. Keep on this to the next gate and then down and round the hillside, till it makes a sharp left turn and heads down to some farm buildings.

Initially walk down towards these farm buildings, but when you meet the fence on your right, turn right and walk along it, keeping the fence to your left. This will bring you through a gateway onto a more recogniazable track across the next field. Walk across this to the gateway into the next field. Here the track disappears again, and you cling to the hillside of this steep field, heading for the tall tree on the far side, on roughly the same line as you've been walking. Near this tree you will find a stile out onto the open hillside. Across this, take the left-hand path which slants downhill to the wood below. When you meet the wood you've come to the last of the awkward crossings.

Below you you should be able to see a bridge across the stream, and you want to cross the fence here, follow the rough path through the wood and cross the bridge. Over this the path heads to the bottom left-hand corner of the wood to the right up the hillside opposite. Then it follows the edge of the wood, keeping it to your right, and at the top, bears more to the right to leave the field by a gate just to the right of the farm and its buildings. Cross a little field in front of the farmhouse to another gate. Through this you are back on a minor road. Turn left on this and walk down it towards Cregrina. When you reach a road junction, turn right to return to your vehicle.

GLASCWM

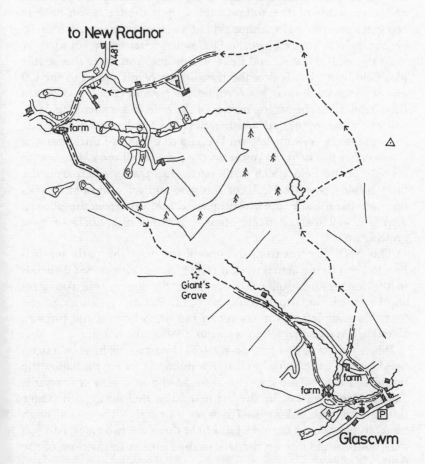

Two and a half hours

A walk largely on tracks, some paths and a short section of A road
which has a wide grassy verge. The walk traverses fields and open hil-
side, with wide views especially to the north and west. There are two
long but not particularly steep ascents.

Park near the triangle of roads at the centre of the village.

Walk down the road leading downhill from where you've parked, going straight ahead on the track at the bend. Keep on this track as it clambers uphill and passes a farm off to your left. When you reach a point roughly adjacent to the end of the buildings on your left, and where a line of trees follows a fence up to the track, you come to two gates on your right, either side of a fence rising up the hillside. Go through the nearest gate, and follow the fence up on your left.

At the end of the second field on this line, you enter the middle of a field by a gate. Follow the track which bends round to the left and serves a small quarry. Go round the bottom of the quarry and then head up to the far top corner of the field to another gate. Here you enter the corner of another field, and walk ahead diverging from the fence on your left but keeping to the left of the summit of the slope in the field. As you cross the field you'll see a gate on the far side of the field which leads out to two tracks which cross the open hillside beyond. Head for this gate and once through it, take the right-hand track which continues to lead up across the hillside. This is a well marked track, often with rushy hummocks of grass growing on it.

This track diverges from the line of the definitive path, but it is best to keep to the actual track on the ground. This presently bends to the left towards some forestry. Near the fence here you meet another track, on which you turn right. Follow this all along the fence on your left to the corner of the fields beyond the forestry, round which you turn left to once more follow the fence.

When you come to a gate on the left, almost at the head of a steep sided cwm in the hillside, go through this and turning to shadow the right-hand side of the cwm, go through the next gate a few yards ahead. Here you rejoin the route of the definitive path. Once through the gate, follow the fence on your right—there is a rough track. In the bottom corner of this field there are two gates, and you walk down to the one on the left, in the fence at the bottom of the field.

Go across the next small field to the gate on the far side, and once through it turn left to follow the fence and hedge on your left. Further on you enter a field by a gate to find the hedge on your left is now further down the hillside below you. Walk roughly parallel to this hedge, again there is the course of a track through the field, and you eventually come to a gate in a pointed corner of the field. Go through this gate and you pick up a more major track which you now follow down till it meets a metalled lane.

Carry on ahead on this lane till it makes a sharp bend to the right. At this corner, go through the gate ahead, and the path follows the field boundary on your left. This will swing round to the right and then to the left and you leave the field by a gate onto another lane. Turn right on this and walk down to the main road.

Turn left on the road and carry on to the sharp bend ahead, where you turn down the track on the left and which leads down to a collection of farm buildings. Bear left to these, turning right past the end of the first building and entering the field behind by the gate. Cross the bottom of this field to the gate on the far side, and through this turn left up the track. This leads between two fields and then along the right-hand edge of another, at the top corner of which it once more leads between fields. Here there is a short slightly overgrown section, but within not too many yards you join another track. Bear left on this track.

Follow the track up to the corner of the wood ahead. Through the gate here you follow the wood on your left to the next fence, at which you turn right and follow it up to the handling area near the crest of the hill. Walk through the handling area to then follow a fence on your right. As you follow this round the hillside you come to a point where there is a limb of the field off to the right. But here you can see a gate on the far side of the field, and you walk across to this. Through the gate you walk up to the mounds on the ridge, called the Giant's Grave. Keep straight on over the ridge and down the other side.

The track eventually meets and shadows a fence on your left. Further on it crosses a small stream and bends to the left, passing through a gate into a field. Here the track becomes fairly sunken and at the far corner of the field passes through another gate into the next. Soon after this the track bends left to cross a stream, but you stay on the near side of the stream to the gates above the stream. Go through the first gate onto a stoned track, which bends left at the top of the field. Keep on this track, and it will lead you down to a farm, where you bear left once past the new barn and walk down to a road. Turn left on this to return to your vehicle.

HERGEST RIDGE & GLADESTRY

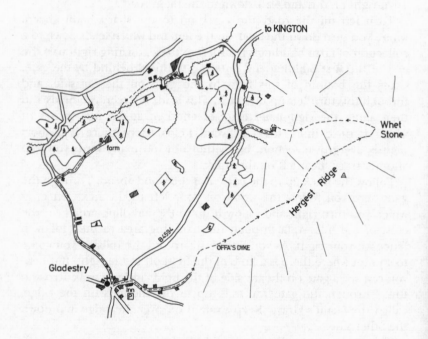

Two and a quarter hours.

A walk on good quality tracks and paths, including a section of Offa's Dyke path over Hergest Ridge, with good views, rolling countryside, open hillside, woods and streams.

Park at or near the Royal Oak in Gladestry.

From outside the pub turn right on the road and almost immediately right again on the minor road. Offa's Dyke path is soon signposted off to the left; take this following a good track past some houses and then through a gate out onto Hergest Ridge. Keep to Offa's Dyke path, ascending the hill in stages and passing a triangulation pillar away to the right. Just before you reach the summit, Offa's Dyke path meets a broad grassy track and you bear left on this. As

72

you circle the summit watch for the Whetstone on your right—a not particularly large rock a few yards into the vegetation.

Here, making a hairpin left turn from the track you've just been walking along, is a smaller track heading downhill and aiming to the left-hand edge of Hanter Hill. Take this track, crossing the pass between Hergest Ridge and Hanter Hill, shortly after which the track bends left and follows a fence. Carry on downhill, the track gradually swinging right and becoming more of a path. It will lead you above a house, your route then turning left and crossing an old stile adjacent to one of the gates in front of and to the side of an old barn. The path then crosses in front of the house and you walk down the track which leads from the house to the B road in the valley bottom.

On the road turn right and adjacent to the first field you come to on the left, turn left up a small path and cross a stile into the field. (The end of the path is marked by a public footpath post which has no sign!) The path now slants across the field to a stile on the far side into the wood ahead. Cross this stile, the path then slanting right, up and across the hillside in the wood. Cross the track you come to almost immediately in the wood, and towards the top of the hill, the path bends left to a stile on the far side. Cross this stile and then diagonally cross the field you're in to the far left-hand corner. You'll see a gate as you approach, and cross this to emerge onto a path on the other side. This path initially follows a gully on your right, before bearing half left and dropping down to a stream in the valley bottom. Cross this by the footbridge provided, go through the gate ahead, and then turn left at the road junction not many yards further on.

Walk on along this road till you come to a gate across it to a house. Go through this. Bear left shortly afterwards to keep to the left of the house and follow a new fence on the left which runs alongside the track. This will bring you to a gate at the far end; once through you keep straight ahead and this will lead you back onto a track. Turn left on this and cross the stream either by the footbridge or the ford. Follow the track from the ford to the wood ahead and then to the right. This leads across the hillside to a gate into a field. Once through this the track zig-zags up the hillside to a farm. Go through the gate into the farmyard, in which you keep right to leave it by another gateway. Walk down the track you're now on between two hedges before entering a field, when you continue to keep to the track as it stays close to the hedge on your left. Through the gateway at the far end the track will lead you past a house to a crossroads. Turn left here onto a lane and this will lead you back to Gladestry.

HERROCK HILL

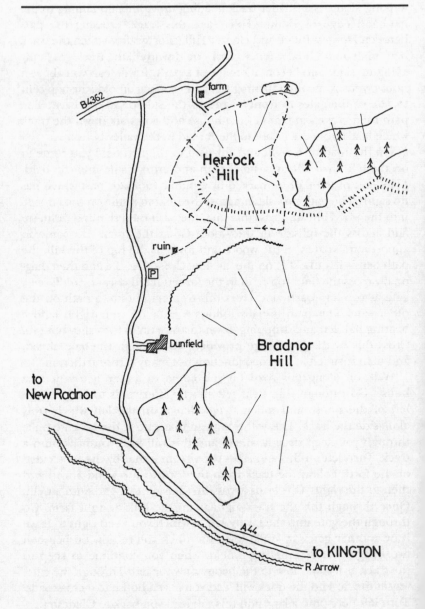

One hour.

This walk incorporates part of Offa's Dyke path, with views over the hills around Kington, and the valley of the Hindwell Brook. It is all on major tracks, and there is one long but not too arduous ascent to make.

Take the A44 west out of Kington and take the first minor road on the right which is signposted to Dunfield House and Dunfield Farm. Follow this road, bearing left at the farm driveway, to the top of the rise which you come to quite suddenly, and park here.

On your right as you come to the top of the rise in the road there is a gate which you go through and then follow the track which keeps to the hedge and fences on your left. This track soon comes to the remains of a ruined building at which point the path turns slightly left and crosses a field to a gate at the foot of Herrock Hill. Go through the gate and then turn left along a sunken track and follow it round the hillside.

Towards the far side of the hill a track leads down down to the left to some farm buildings—ignore this and carry on round the hill, keeping the fence to your left. A little further on another track joins yours from the left—this is Offa's Dyke path. Carry on walking along round the hill, now following the Offa's Dyke path and the acorn waymarking signs. A little further on you come to two gates and Offa's Dyke path is waymarked through the right-hand gate. Past some farm buildings the path divides again, and again it is the right-hand path you take, slanting up the side of the hill. At the crest of the hill Offa's Dyke path is signposted to the left; you should continue straight on down the far side of the hill. This will lead you to an elbow of fencing, in the far corner of which is a gate. Turn right onto the track which leads back to the gate at the foot of the hill. You then return to your vehicle by the same route as you approached the hill.

HERGEST RIDGE
& HERGEST CROFT GARDENS

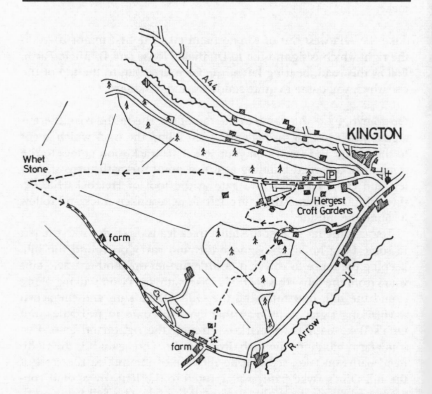

An hour and a half.

This walk involves a very gradual ascent of Hergest Ridge on lanes and tracks to give fine views of the countryside in all directions. The return journey, largely on paths and some lane, includes views over Hergest Court and a footpath which crosses some of the rhododendron and azalea woods of Hergest Croft gardens.

You can start the walk from Kington, or drive and park in the car park at Hergest Croft Gardens. From the centre of Kington, drive or walk uphill towards and past the church, turning left on to the road to the gardens just over the brow of the hill. Carry on till you reach the car park on the right. Park here if still in a car!

From the car park carry on walking up the lane which will soon lead you out on to the open hillside of Hergest Ridge. Keep to the left-hand wide track once on the hillside and this will eventually lead you up to the first and lower summit. Near here a small clump of coni-fers have been planted, just before you reach an area of gorse, and you want to take a fairly indistinct path which makes a hair pin bend left. (The whetstone, a reasonably large single stone should be off to the right set in the gorse. This gained its name when, during the reign of Edward III, the inhabitants of Kington suffered from an out-break of disease. To try and avoid catching the disease, the neigh-bouring inhabitants brought their wheat—hence the name whet—to this stone where they left it, returning later to collect their payment.)

The path shadows a fairly deep and prominent gully running out from the ridge on your right, and as you gently descend the hillside you cross a track and the path itself becomes a track. You now approach a farm, your route passing to its right, joining the lane which serves it. Carry on down this for a while till you meet another road at a sharp bend just by another farm. At this junction, just past the last of the buildings on the left, you turn left up a track. But don't stay on this for more than a few paces, crossing the stile to the left of a gate almost immediatley on your right, and in front of an old castle mound. Now turn left to follow the hedge on your left.

Keep following this, crossing three stiles before you find yourself having entered the middle of a field. Here the path turns half right and crosses the field. As you cross over and slightly downhill you'll see a stile on the far side. Cross this and you enter Park Wood, where some of the rhododendron collection grows. The path, or rather track, soon bends left and passes in front of a pool, before continu-ing through the woodland to a cottage, where it bends to the left, shortly to leave the wood.

Outside the wood initially carry on ahead but after some thirty yards you meet a track running across your's on which you turn left, to shadow the stream on your left. When you come adjacent to a pond, marked by some trees on the near bank, turn sharp right and slightly back on yourself to walk up towards the wall and house. Follow the wall and pass in front of the house to the kissing gate which leads into an avenue of trees. Walk down this for a hundred yards or so, before bearing half left and crossing the azalea walk on your left and entering an area of young trees. Here you should be able to make out a gate leading out on to a lane, for which you make.

Turn right on the lane to return to your vehicle—or Kington.

A note on Kington

Harold Godwinson took the land and town for himself after quashing a rising by the local inhabitants who had joined in a Welsh raid on Hereford. Thus at the time of the Domesday Survey in 1086 the manor was in royal hands, though still classified as waste land due to the warfare.

Henry I granted the manor to Adam de Port in 1108 with the intention of creating a major castle and probably a borough. But the only known record of the castle is in 1186 when repairs to the palisade are mentioned. The castle, or more likely fortified watch tower from this reference, was abandoned around 1230 when the nearby settlement of Huntington had a borough marked out, though this plan was never actually fulfilled.

By 1267 the area was in the hands of the de Bohun family, and the town was starting to grow, spreading down the hill towards the area where its centre now lies.

The church was probably founded in the 1100's, though the earliest surviving part is the tower which was originally detached from the rest of the church, providing a place of refuge for the town's citizens. There is a fine early thirteenth century chancel, and the church contains the tomb of Thomas Vaughan and his wife Ellen. He fought on the Yorkist side in the Wars of the Roses and was killed at the Battle of Banbury in 1469. Ellen was given the name of 'Gethin', meaning the terrible, for when in her teens she attended an archery tournament at which she shot her brother's murderer. Their home was Hergest Court which is reputed to be haunted by a black bloodhound, a tale which forms the basis for Conan Doyle's *Hound of the Baskervilles*.

To the west of Kington lies Hergest Ridge, included in this walk, and on which lies the Whetstone. This has been reputed to go down to drink in the stream below the ridge every morning that it hears a cock crow.

On the lower slopes lie Hergest Croft Gardens, which include a large rhododendron and azalea collection, together with the national collection of maples and birches.

CWMMAU FARMHOUSE

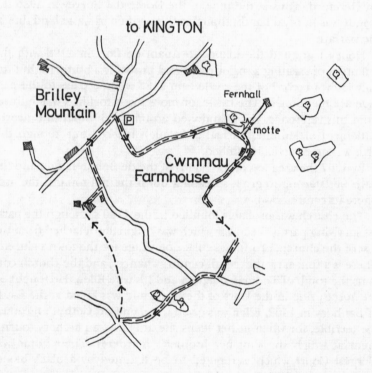

One hour.

A walk with views towards Merebach Hill and the Black Mountains further west and passing through the farmyard at the National Trust farm of Cwmmau. A walk on a mixture of paths, tracks and minor road, where one track is fairly overgrown.

From Kington take the road out of town from opposite the church. Keep on the mainer of the roads, crossing the River Arrow, passing by an old army camp, before generally rising towards Brilley Mountain. You want to park after passing some houses and farms to first right and then left, and just beyond a junction with another road and a lane and where Cwmmau Farm is signposted.

Walk up the lane signposted to Cwmmau Farm, this presently bending to the left. Further on it crosses a cattle grid, and later still you start to curve to the right above Cwmmau Farm. Keep right at a junction of tracks and carry on along the track through the farmyard at Cwmmau. Don't dally too long, for remember it is a working farm.

Continue on the main track through the farmyard, which means taking the left-hand option of the choices of two gates that are sometimes offered. At the end of a passage between two fields, the track bears sharp left through a small gate, and still you follow a route between two hedges. This is where the track can start to become slightly obstructed. Soon you start to pass fields of blackcurrants on your left, and dropping downhill you half enter one of these fields. But here the track bears sharp right and soon leads out onto a minor road.

Turn right and walk along the road, continuing straight on past a turning off to the right, till you reach a T-junction. Here there is a stile bedded in the hedge on your right at the corner. If this is still overgrown, turn right on the road at the T-junction to the first gate on your right, and walk through this into the field. Then walk towards the top far corner of the field, passing through a gate here into the field above it. Follow the hedge round on your right and over the brow of the hill to the far right corner, keeping the old barns well to your left.

Over the old gate in this corner, again follow the hedge on your right to the top right-hand corner, here passing out over some rails onto a farm track. Walk through the farmyard on this track, bearing right at the house, and down to a road. Turn left on this, and right at the T-junction further on to return to your vehicle.

SNODHILL

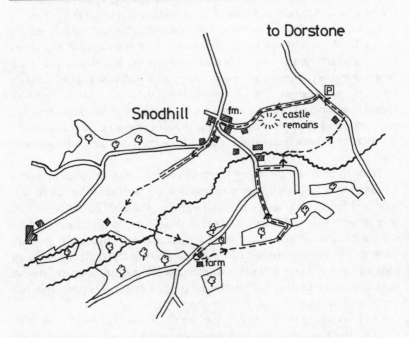

One hour.

A walk on a mixture of very minor roads, tracks and paths in rolling countryside with wide views and passing the remains of Snodhill Castle. This was the home of the Chandos family who fought alongside the Black Prince in France. Most of the going is fairly gentle, though there is one longish ascent.

From Dorstone on the B4348 initially follow the signs to Snodhill, heading south from the village on minor roads, not the B road. At the edge of the village go straight ahead on the road signposted to Peterchurch, not right to Snodhill. About a mile out park where suitable at the next junction with a minor road on the right.

Turn right up the minor road at this junction, and on the left you pass Snodhill Castle. (There are better views of it later on.) Continue along the road till you reach a crossroads, which you cross to go onto the lane marked 'no through road'. This bends to the left and soon comes to a couple of cottages bang next door to each other on the right. Here you leave the road and bear left on to a track which leads through a wood, still generally following the direction in which you've just been walking. Keep through the wood and into a field beyond. The track now follows the fence on your right to the entrance into the next field. Here the line of the track, if you look hard for it, bears slightly away from this fence to a gate on the far side of the field, just below a cottage on the hillside. As you cross this field, look out for the farm on the ridge on your left.

As you reach the gate, bear left, aiming straight for the farm just mentioned. Your route will take you down across a stream and through some gateways, then up the far side to the left-hand corner of a wood and finally into a small field. Here you should soon see the chimney stack of the farm, and gradually more of the building as you breast the rise. Leave the field by the gate in front of the farm, turning right on to the lane. Some fifty yards past the farm, turn left up a short track and enter a field near an old stone barn. Here turn left down the hedge, keeping the barn to your right. When the hedge drops away to your left, keep just to the left of the high knoll ahead, passing into the field beyond by a stile-cum-hurdle. You now roughly keep following the same line, walking across the next field to a gate on the far side. Then shadow the wood on your left to a gate at the far left-hand corner of the field. Go through this and once more you join a track. Keep to this across the rough patch of ground, and presently a major track leads off sharp left downhill. Turn on to this and follow it down to the lane at the bottom. The remains of Snodhill Castle are now just to the right of straight ahead, and you should be able to make out some of the walling of the old keep.

On the lane turn right, then take the track off to the right shortly before you reach some buildings. Follow this for a few hundred yards till it makes a gentle bend to the right and becomes more overgrown. Here you turn through a gate on your left to cross a small field to the gate on the far side. Through this turn right to follow the hedges and fences on your right. At the corner of the field you follow fences round to the left and enter the next paddock through a gateway. Through this, turn right down the fence and pass through the gate in the dip at the foot of the field into the field below. Now follow the hedge on your left up towards a cottage, passing out of the field to its right and on to a minor road. Turn left to return to your vehicle.

CUSOP

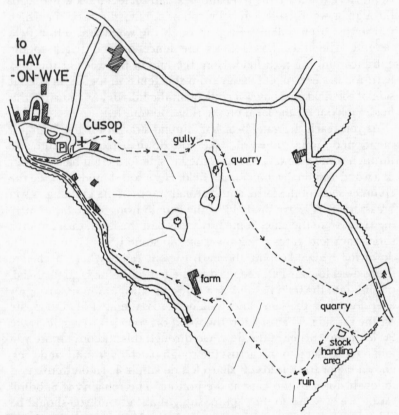

Two hours.

A very pleasant walk over hillsides with views over the border country. Mainly on paths across fields and hillside and which aren't well defined, but also some tracks and small sections of minor road.

Park near the church in Cusop.

Walk through the churchyard to the right of the church to the gate at the far end. Turn right in the field and follow its boundary on your right to the gate ahead. Through the gate bear left to follow the field boundary and deep rutted track on your right round the next corner. From this corner head up the hillside across the corner of the field to another gate. Through this gate the path bears left above the gully and angles up across the hillside to a number of gates in the far corner of the field. Go through the gate on the right, and the path now bears to the right climbing and diagonally crossing the next patch of ground. When it flattens out slightly you can see the remains of old quarry workings on the skyline. The path ascends this by a brief section of track after which you follow the edge of the slope on your right, continuing to ascend and curve round the hillside. Presently you'll come to some fences, in the corner of which a stile leads over into the next enclosure.

Bear slightly to the left once over this stile, continuing to ascend the hill, reaching another stile in the next fence. Cross this and carry on for a while on the same line, and when you near a second batch of old quarry workings on your right and a metal gate at the foot of a clump of trees lies to your immediate left, the path turns left and heads to the gate through which it passes onto a minor road.

Turn right on the road and right again through the next gate on the right into the following field. Head to the left of the trees which mark the site of a spring and follow the watercourse down till you join a track which follows the emergent stream. At this point you are adjacent to some rough ground on your immediate left. Cross the stream and head over the field, ascending slightly, to a gate above a stock handling area. Pass through this gate onto a plateau-like field. In the woodland on the left you'll see a track which slants down the hillside, following a cleft on your left. Take this track and it will lead you down to a couple of wrecked cottages and barns. Beyond these lie a fence and a gate. Here the path turns right before the fence and you follow it on your left to a stile at the next fence. Cross this and, bearing slightly left, continue following the fence on your left through some bracken, this path soon becoming better defined and swinging right to more parallel the contours of the hillside.

Follow this path, taking the path off to the left when you emerge onto more open hillside, and drop down to the hedge below. Follow this to the gate in the corner. Through the gate follow the field boundary on your left to the next field which the path then crosses to meet a track leading into a farmyard. Keep on the track, passing the farmhouse to your right and it gains a metalled surface as it bears left and downhill to join a minor road. Turn right on the road. When the road meets another on the right after a piece of conifer wood, bear sharp right onto it and follow it back to your vehicle.

LLOWES

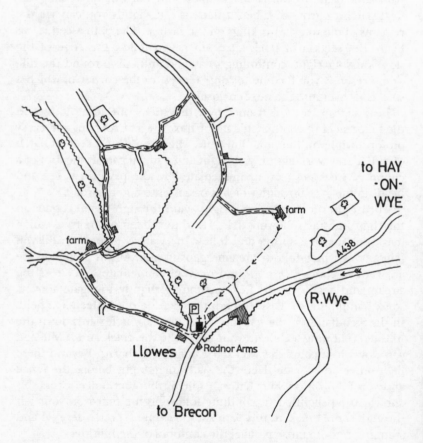

One and a quarter hours.

A walk largely on main tracks and very minor metalled lanes, with views as you descend over the Wye Valley between Hay and Glasbury, with the Black Mountains beyond.

In Llowes turn away from the Wye opposite the Radnor Arms, and then almost immediately right to park near the church.

Walk on up the lane away from the Radnor Arms. You pass one turning to the left and further on a house on your right immediately on the road. Past this the road bends to the left and here you take the drive off to the right. This leads down past a farm and alongside a brook, before turning left up the hillside. Past the next set of buildings on your right the drive becomes a track. Keep following this up the hillside, and where it divides further ahead, take the right-hand turn. Further on it meets a surfaced track, and you turn left onto this (in essence to carry on walking roughly on the same line ahead) and this soon gains a metalled surface.

You pass a farm on the right and the lane still keeps gently ascending round a series of bends. Then it bears sharp right where a track leaves to the left, and starts to gently descend the hillside. You pass two tracks off to the left, one with a bungalow on your left and part of its garden to your right at the junction.

Take the third track off to the left, this leading you to a gate into some rough grazing. Walk on down the track to the farm ahead, bearing right through the farmyard, keeping all the main buildings to your left. On the far side of the farmyard you pass alongside one field at the end of which the semi-sunken track turns left, but you take the footpath through the gate ahead. This follows the hedge on your right to a stile at the next field boundary. Over this you pick up the course of another track which leads rather more through the field and through the woodland on the far side after which it heads straight for Llowes Church. Near the end of this last field it swings left and leaves through the gates in the bottom far corner. Return to your vehicle through the churchyard.

Refreshment can of course be had at the Radnor Arms.

LLANIGON

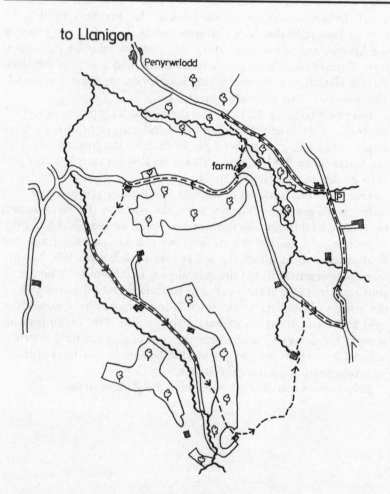

to Llanigon

Penyrwrlodd

farm

P

One and three-quarter hours.

A walk on a mixture of lanes, tracks and paths with a couple of awkward fence crossings. To compensate there are views with a difference of the flanks of the Black Mountains and over the Welsh borders, and a section of stream to follow. The route is fairly up and down, but there are no long steep ascents involved.

From Hay take the B4350 to Glasbury, taking the first left out of the town onto the fairly wide minor road signposted to Llanigon. Almost as soon as you enter the village you come to the Old Forge Garage on your left, and you turn left immediately past it onto a narrow road. This winds through the French-like Penyrwrlodd Farm, and you carry on till you meet another road, almost a mile further on. Park near this junction.

Walk back down the road you've just driven along. Initially there are fields to your right, whilst you pass clumps of woodland on your left. But almost as soon as you also reach woodland on your right, you turn sharp left almost back on yourself on to a wide grassy track. This soon enters out into a sort of clearing, where you keep to the top of the bank on the right and soon meet a narrow path which leads down to the stream below, coming out above a small waterfall. Cross the stream as soon as you can and follow it till you come to the end of a newly formed track which leads down to the stream from your right. Walk up this, and turn left at the top of the bank, to walk up the field, heading slightly to the left of the farm on the slope above.

As you near the farm, you'll meet a track leading down from the farm and you turn right on to this following it up to the buildings. However, don't go through the gateway into the farmyard, for the path bears right, follows the buildings then on your left, crosses a hurdle at the fence ahead, and keeps on the same line across the next field till you come adjacent to a gate on your left, when you turn left and go through the gate on to a lane.

Turn right on the lane, and follow it along the foot of the wood on your left. Not far beyond the end of the wood you reach a house on the left which is approached by passing under part of a barn. Here you turn left, pass under the barn and leave the yard by the gate ahead and to the right of the house. Follow the track through the next field to the next gate. Through this, you turn slightly more to the right and head for the far right-hand corner of this quite large field. In the corner you will find one of the awkward fences to cross, and you want to end up in the woodland below the field you've just crossed. Having achieved this, aim to the left of where the lane beyond the woodland crosses the stream, and here you will find a gate out onto the lane.

Turn left on this lane and follow it uphill. When it reaches a couple of houses on the right, it loses its metalled surface and becomes a track. Keep on this track for a reasonable distance, but as soon as it crosses a little stream, beyond which there is gate ahead into a field whilst the track turns slightly to the right, go through that gate into the field in front of you. Initally shadow the hedge on your left, but when you reach its corner, turn half left and walk up to the far left-hand corner of the field. Here you will find a gate onto another track, which slolwy climbs uphill through woodland. It eventually reaches a fence near the wreck of an old building. Now the best route is to cross this fence by the stile provided, and then follow it on your left uphill and unobstructed to the top left-hand corner of the field, where you have another fence to cross, though there are some corner posts to help in this.

Once into the narrow field beyond, walk along the line of the old track, shadowing the fence on your left, and then round the corner and up to a gate in top right-hand corner. Through this, turn left along the line of old fence posts, then round to the right and left at the field boundary ahead. This will bring you to an old stone construction, which is a sheep dip. Go through the gate to the immediate right of this into a field, then walk down this field aiming to the left of a Dutch barn. Here you'll find a track which leads into the farmyard, and your route leads you to the left of the house and through a gate to then pass in front of it. Walk straight ahead from this gate, crossing a small stream and up the bank on the other side to leave the yard by a gate into a field. In this field, carry on walking on the same line, keeping to the hedge on your immediate right. This will bring you into the next field where you'll soon see another house beyond it. Aim to the left of this house and you cross a stile and emerge onto a steep bank. Walk along the top of this, eventually dropping down it to a gate at the far end and passing out onto a lane.

Turn right on the lane and at the next junction, left to return to your vehicle.

CASTELL DINAS

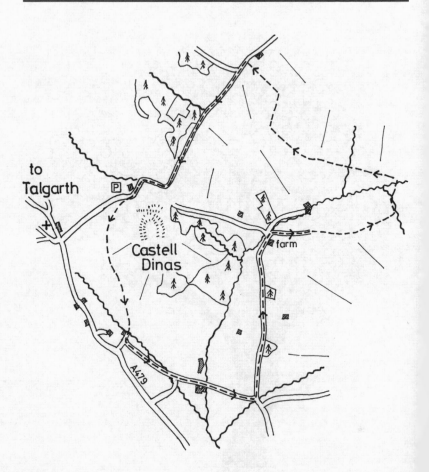

Two hours.

A walk on paths, tracks and minor roads at the foot of and along the lower slopes of the Black Mountains. It involves two separate clambers of some 400 feet height, the second to cross a small pass in a shoulder of the mountains with views in several directions. Castell Dinas, a well marked hillfort is circuited, and a rather battered long cairn passed.

Take the A479 from Talgarth to Abergavenny. This climbs up to pass between the Black Mountains on the left and Mynydd Troed on the right. As it starts to near the summit between these hills you first pass a staggered crossroads with two minor roads, and then another road off to the left. Almost immediately after this you pass a telephone box on the left and you want to take the small lane off to the left some hundred yards beyond this telephone box. (If you reach the Castle Inn on the main road, you've gone a touch too far.) Drive down the lane till you come to a parking area on the right. This is just before the continuation of the lane to the right is signposted as a public path, and before a drive leads off straight ahead to a house. You want to park in this area.

Immediately before this parking area is a gate on the same side of the lane. Go through this, with Castell Dinas on your left, and walk along the line of the old track which you can just about make out, to the gate on the far side of the field. Through this cross the next field on much the same line to a stile on the far side, and over this similarly cross the next field to the next gateway. Once through this you enter a longer field, and the path now bears to the far right-hand corner, where it bends to the right and more steeply downhill through the next field to a gateway above the stream in the valley bottom. Through this follow the stream on your right to the ford ahead, passing over it and up the far side to emerge onto a lane. Turn left on this and follow it back across the stream further on to a minor road.

Turn left on this, and as you cross the highest point in a few hundred yards, the battered long cairn lies on the top of the hillock on your right. Carry on along this road, passing a riding stables and follow it up to a T-junction. Turn left here and keep on this road into a farmyard. Immediately before the road crosses the stream in front of the farmhouse, you turn right, essentially keeping straight ahead, to take a track which starts ro rise up the hillside, shortly bending to the right.

Keep on this track, which passes between fields to left and right, before emerging on the open hillside. Here turn left and almost immediately half right on a grassy path which continues slanting across the hillside. It soon reaches a clump of wind battered trees, and here you turn left to the corner of the fields below you, then following the field boundary on your left down towards the stream in the valley bottom. Before you reach this, the path bears slightly to the right, then crosses the stream after which you turn left to keep following the field boundaries on your left.

When you're roughly adjacent to an old railway carriage used as a stock shelter in the valley floor to your right, you want to take the path which starts to rise slightly to the right, slanting across the hillside to the saddle in the ridge on your right. This path later turns right to head straight at the saddle, over which it turns right and slants downhill. When you're just about above the farm on your left this path meets a track sloping downhill from the right, and you turn left on this and head towards the little gate out onto a minor road to the left of a small wood. Once through this gate, turn left and go through the larger gate back onto the hillside. Now follow the wide track which shadows field boundaries on your right, and as you near Castell Dinas once more, it turns sharp right, to pass through a gateway. Just follow this track as it later bends left and right again, and it will lead you to your vehicle.

LLANFILO

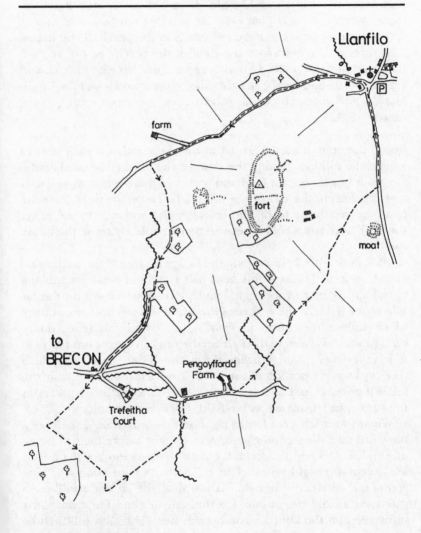

One and a half hours.

Starting from the interesting church at Llanfilo, this walk is on a mix of minor roads, tracks and paths. Set in rolling wooded countryside, it has views to the north across the valley of the Dulas, and also towards the east and the flank of the Black Mountains. There is an early climb of some 250 feet, but then it's easy going.

Park near the church at Llanfilo. Recently this church has been locked when I've visited, but even the outside is worth a look, with its carved window lintels, and carved stones in the porch. If you have a look through the window to the right of the porch you can also see the magnificently carved rood screen. This has vine leaves and grapes, bosses and heads, and carvings of the apostles and the Virgin Mary. The figures above the rood screen are more recent, being carved in 1925.

Above the church take the road to the right and you soon start to ascend the hillside, gaining the views to the north. The road gradually leads out onto open land and presently flattens out. As you start a gentle descent there is a drive off to a house on the right. Take the first gate you come to on the left after the entrance to the drive, shortly before you would otherwise be immediately above the house itself.

Walk down this field, keeping the hedge on your right, to the gate at the bottom. Through this bear half right and head towards the right-hand corner of the right-hand piece of woodland on the far side of the field. At the corner of this wood you will find an old track which follows the fence on your right. Follow this fence down, though you may need to divert from the track in one or two places as it is fairly overgrown. Further down the hillside you will join a recently re-made portion of the track. Turn left on this, initially still following fences and a stream on your right, then the track crosses the stream and heads across two fields towards some houses.

When you reach a road, turn right on this and within a matter of a few yards take the second gate on the left, just before the first house on the left. Once in this field, the path shadows the hedge on your left, keeping roughly parallel to it, so that you're almost walking across the middle of the field. As you near the far end you'll see a gate near an old tree stump. Go through this and for about thirty yards keep on the same line across this next field. You will then be adjacent to a gate into a field on your right, and here you want to make a near right-angled turn left onto the line of an old track. This will lead towards a clump of trees and a gateway into the next field. Go through this gateway and walk down the same line, now clearly (on a clear day!) heading towards the flank of the Black Mountains.

Once through the gate on the far side of this field, follow the track sharp round to the right to another gate. Immediately through this, cross into the point of the field on your left by the gate. Then follow the hedge on your left, passing through a gate ahead into the next field. Again follow the hedge on your left, and when you come to a gate in this, go through it, bear marginally more to the left of the general line on which you've been walking to the stream ahead, crossing it by a bridge and heading to the gate which leads onto an old track between hedgerows. Walk up this and past a barn to the road ahead.

Turn right on the road and walk up to Pengoyffordd Farm on the left. Immediately past the old barn at this farm, go through the gate on your left. Again shadow the fence on your left to the gate you should be able to see just over the small rise on the far side of the field. Go through this gate, and cross the next field to the gate below you. Through this turn right and go through the gate immediately on your right. In this next field turn left and cross up it to the far right-hand corner. Here you will find a track bewteen the wood and the fields on your right, and you follow this and it heads up and then slightly right to a gate into another field. Go through this gate and cross the limb of the field on your right to the corner of hedge and fence ahead of you. Turn left and walk along this to the gate in the far corner of the field. Go through this and turn slightly right to walk across to the gate into the next field. Through this gate, head to the bottom far corner of the field, and the entrance to yet another field. Again, once through this, head to the gate in the far left-hand corner, this gate leading out onto a track, which itself immediately leads onto a road. Turn left on the road to return to your vehicle.

CRICKADARN

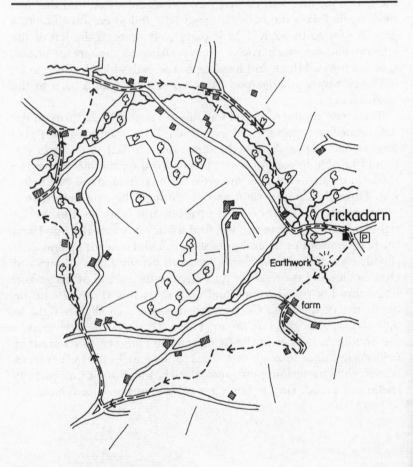

One and three-quarter hours.

A walk in pleasant rolling countryside on lanes, tracks and paths. It passes the motte remains of Crickadarn Castle, has comparatively wide views and returns by a wide stream, old oak wood and a derelict water mill. Parts of the walk can be quite boggy, so pay heed to footwear, and there are a couple of less than convenient fence crossings, though these have been reported to the county council and so could be cleared up by now.

Park by the church in Crickadarn.

The route sets off by passing through the gate to the immediate left of the one into the churchyard, leaving the garden at the rear of the house by another gate. In the right-hand corner of the patch of ground beyond there is a stile into the next field. Follow the hedge on your right, and then the ditch till you come to a bridge across it. Go over this, and then keep to the left of the old castle mound, heading into the far left-hand corner of the field. In the undergrowth here you will find the remains of an old track and a fence to cross into the field beyond. Here you head for the bottom-right of the steep bank ahead, where you will find a stile in the hedge. Cross this and then follow the line of the old path across the next field to a stile out onto the lane beyond.

Turn left on the lane, and as you reach the farm ahead, turn right onto the track off to the right. This passes by some new barns, then swings left and curves round the hillside. (There are good views over the old castle site from this track.) The track will lead you up to a gate in the top corner of the field, but you turn right immediately in front of it and follow the hedge on your left all the way along to the next far corner of the field.

Here you will find two gateways, and you take the left-hand one, but then keep to much the same line, following the hedge on your right. This will lead you to a gate onto a track, which you take. When the track bends right to descend to a farm, you bear half-left to follow a track through a rushocky field, keeping near to a hedge on your left. This will lead you to a gate in the corner of the field, through which you pass to then follow the hedge on your right to another gate. Through this you again keep to the hedge on your right, though now you are on more open hillside with a fair amount of bracken. Keep shadowing the hedge and you will come to a metalled lane. Cross this, walking up the hillside opposite and when the track which you join comes to a gateway into a field, in fact the second field above the lane, go through this gate onto the track beyond. Walk down this and out of the gate at the far end onto another metalled lane.

Go across the crossroads here, and round to the right at the bend ahead. Beyond the bend, look out for a stile plcaed almost side on at the first junction with a hedge leading off to the left. Cross this interesting stile, and initially follow the hedge on your right, but cross the stream once you reach it. Now walk along the bank above the

99

stream, and eventually you will have to cross a fence into some rough woodland at the end of the field. Keep close to the stream and you will join a track which comes down from the left. Bear right on the track and it will lead you past some old barns, before curving round to the left. When the currently used track turns right through a gate, the path keeps on the old track between the hedges, crosses a stream and then enters a farmyard by a gate at almost the same point as the stream does!

Turn right on the lane at the end of which you find yourself. Having crossed a stream the lane divides, and you take the left-hand split. Walk up the slope beyond and when the lane bends left, you turn right onto a track. Keep to this track, which turns left not far ahead; further on becomes more of a path, though still set between hedges, and then bends right and left in quick succession before once more becoming wider and dropping down to a road.

Turn right on the road and follow it along to a cattle grid entry to a farm on your left. Cross the cattle grid, and bear left up the track to the farm. At the bend on the track, go through the gate into the field ahead, turning right to follow the hedge on your right to the corner of the field. Cross the stile here and cross the next field to the gate on the far side. Through this walk below the house to take a gate on your left beyond it and onto the farm drive. Turn right on the drive, which soon makes a sharp turn left. In front of you at this bend are two gates. Take the left-hand one and walk along the track, which will lead into and through some woodland. On the far side of the wood, continue following the wood on your left to its corner, then strike across the field aiming for a point some twenty yards down from the corner of the wood opposite. Here you will find a little path which leads through the oak wood. The further you walk through the wood, the more paths there seem to be, and you want to gradually descend towards the stream, to a point a little beyond a small bend it makes. Here you will find a footbridge across to the dilapidated mill on the far side. The path now technically leads up the old sunken track and out onto the road, but if this is still obstructed, then you need to take the little gate into the field on the left, walk up to the gate near the top right-hand corner and through the gate beyond that and onto the road.

Turn left on the road to return to your vehicle.

PONT-FAEN

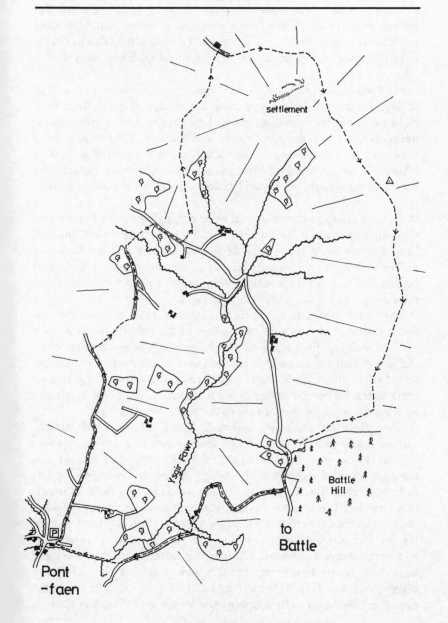

settlement

Ysgir Fawr

Battle
Hill

to
Battle

Pont
-faen

Two hours.

A walk largely on a mixture of lanes, and tracks, with some paths. Set in rolling countryside with sweeping views, especially towards the Brecon Beacons and Black Mountains. There is one quite wide river to ford, so be prepared with footwear. There are hillsides to climb, but the rises are fairly gentle, except for one short sharp ascent.

From Brecon, start to leave the city centre heading west on the road to Llandovery, but before you cross the bridge over the Usk, turn right on the minor road signposted to Cradoc and a golf course. Keep on this road through Cradoc and Battle to Pont-faen, a small village set in a narrowing of the valley and at the foot of a forestry plantation on the left. You can park near the telephone kiosk in the centre of the village, just to the left of the road you're driving along.

Walk back down to the road you were driving along, and cross it to then walk up the lane on the far side. This quickly turns left, and you keep on this for some way as as it curls up the hillside, before it makes a temporary descent. Here the tarmac runs out and mud begins, but you turn through the gate on your right to follow an old rutted track along the hedge on your right.

This track passes through more gateways, takes a more definite form, descends the hillside and swings to the left. It crosses a track off to the right which leads to a farm and continues slanting across the hillside till you came to a pair of gates on your right, either side of a hedge which leads down to the river. Go through the first of these gates, follow the hedge down to the river which you ford, and walk up the track on the far side to the road ahead.

Turn right on the road, and walk uphill till you reach an old sunken track on your right which leads down to a barn. Opposite this track, on your left, is a gate into the middle of a field. Go through this and walk up to the hedge opposite, turning to the left once you reach it to walk up to the gate into the next field. Through this gate lies the sharp ascent. Head to the right of the wooded mound diagonally across this field. As you start to reach the fence on the far side you'll see a gateway into the field beyond. Through this you keep to much the same line passing through another two gateways. Your route then turns slightly more to the right to circle the boggy patch which feeds the stream head on your right. As you come over the hillside you will suddenly see a roof and then a cottage to which it belongs, on your half left. Then some sheds will appear to its right, and you aim for these. In front of them you pass through a gate, and then turn right to go through another gate.

Now follow the fence on your left to the next gateway. The next field has a gorse fringe, and you start to circle the banks of Caer fach on your right. Keep following the fence on your left, and your route will start to swing more to the right, shortly after which you enter a field where there are the bank remnants of a fence on your right running parallel to the fence you've been following. Almost straight haead of you you should see a triangulation pillar on the next hilltop. Your route now crosses to the right of this, heading for the gateway in what would be the far right hand-corner of a small rectangular field, if the fence was still existing on your right.

Once through this gate the path now follows a fence on your right for some distance, passing below the triangulation pillar, then below another piece of higher ground on your left, then passing over a stoned section through a boggy patch before starting gently downhill, with the highest ground now just to your right. As you descend you start to near a forestry plantation, eventually emerging into a large field immediatley in front of it.

Here the definitive footpath follows the wall and fence on your left till some 100 yards in front of the wood, when it turns right and joins an old track which shadows a boggy patch of ground to your left on this side of the wood. Pass through the gateway into the next field, but once through, ignore the new track and follow the old one, curving down the hillside to leave the field by a gate onto a minor road near the corner of the wood itself.

Turn left on the road, passing over a stream, beyond which take the first track to the right. This leads down the hillside to a farm. Walk on the tarmac drive to the left of the house, leaving by the farm gate on the left near the far end. Through this, keep to the left-hand gate to follow a slightly overgrown sunken track alongside the hedge on your right. There is only a fairly short section of this before you enter a field by a gate. Follow the line of the old track across this to the gate almost opposite but slightly downhill. Shadow the wood through the next field, but in the one beyond, once the track starts to curve left away from the stream below, take the path which leads downhill, angling towards the stream. Pass through the gate at the bottom corner into the next field, and now you first hug the bank above the stream and then the stream itself. You return to Pont-faen via a pair of kissing gates between a bungalow and the stream.

BRECON & PEN-Y-CRUG

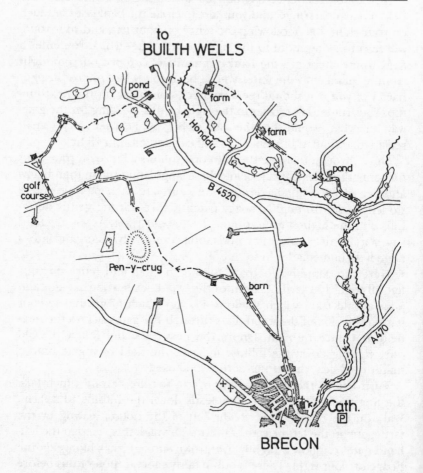

Two and a half hours.

A walk which starts and ends at Brecon Cathedral, which passes Pen-y-crug hillfort with wide sweeping views, passes through woodland and across fields, and by old farm buildings. The last section of the walk is above and by the River Honddu. Largely on good tracks and footpaths, but beware for there is a bridge made from fallen trees to cross where one footbridge has collapsed—unless the county council has since repaired it. Some minor road with wide verges, and two fairly short sections of B road are also involved.

Park at the cathedral.

On the B road by the cathedral walk out of Brecon heading north towards Builth Wells. As you reach the end of the built up area you near road signs indicating the end of speed limits. Before these, and just past the last housing estate on the left, there is a wide gravelled track off to the left. Take this, it almost immediately bending to the right, and walk along as it gradually ascends and passes an old barn on your right. As you near the track's summit, you take a smaller track off to the left which soon makes a small double bend and later enters a yard in front of a house. Here the track becomes a path, keeping to the right in the yard and leads up between two hedge-rows onto the open hillside.

The path is now waymarked, leading initially towards Pen-y-crug, but as you near the foot of the ramparts, swinging to the right to shadow them. It then drops down the hillside to a gate. Go through the gate and follow the path beyond down to a road.

Turn left on the road and walk along it till you come to a golf course. Turn right up the left-hand of the two lanes by the course, bearing right on the lanes when you reach the buildings ahead. This track leads round the edge of the golf course, then through a narrow strip of wood, over a cattle grid and to a farm. Keep right on the tracks immediately in front of the farm buildings, passing down the side of a long, fairly new shed. At the end of this go through a gate to the right of a hedge which continues the line of the shed. Walk down the hedge, and when you come to a gate on your left, go through this. Your route now lies to the left a clump of trees by a little pond in the middle of the field, aiming towards a point where some large boulders are piled up at the edge of the field in front of the woodland on the far side. Here you will find an old gateway partially blocked by fencing, which I hope is still quite easy to cross. Once in the woodland there is a fairly wide path to follow through the wood, and out at the far side onto a metalled lane.

Turn right on this and follow it down to the B road. Turn left on the B road, following it past a small lodge on the left, and on the bends beyond, turn right through a gate immediately before reaching a small stream whch appears to be served by a spring under the road. Follow the stream down to the larger one in the valley bottom, and this is where you may have the awkward crossing over the felled trees. Once across, follow the line of the larger track across the hillside towards the right of the farm just over the rise. Turn left by the buildings and walk through the farmyard. Turn right once past all the buildings—this might either involve passing through some cattle yards next to some new barns, or shadowing the far wall of the silage clamp—take whichever route you prefer!

Once in the field walk across it roughly at right angles to the track you've just left towards the far side, where you'll come to a corner of hedgerow which juts into the field. Keep this to your right and walk down to the gate into the field beyond. Through this keep following the hedge on your right through the next fields, heading towards another farm. Just before you reach it you pass out onto another track, on which you turn right and then left into the wide farmyard, heading for the gate in its far right-hand corner. Through this gate you emerge onto a wide track, which you follow, leading to a gate into another field. Through this you stay following the hedge on your right till you reach more gates. In turn these will lead you into the corner of a much larger field with a large set of new barns diagonally opposite you. Walk just to the right of these to the gate in the far corner of the field, i.e. marginally to the left of the line on which you've just been walking. Through this gate, you turn left on a short track, then right at the junction ahead. This will lead you in an arc round past a pond and by a large pink painted house, then past a wooden bungalow and eventually down to a minor road. (The very last part is not a definitive footpath, but it avoids an awkward stream crossing and the need to walk through what is now a rubbish tip.)

Turn right on the road and once over the stream left across a stile. Over this the path turns up the hillside away from the stream, to eventually pass into the wood above the stream near its top corner. Once over the stile here, the path becomes well worn, and initially keeps to the top of the woodland. Further on it splits, though most of these subsequently rejoin, as it bends to the right to cross a feeder stream, before once more keeping to the top of the wood. Not far beyond this the path becomes wider and many more paths radiate off. The definitive path keeps to the top of the wood till beyond another bend to the right when it drops down towards the river banks near some buildings in a clearing on the far side. Follow the river back into Brecon, passing round a small meadow further on, before coming onto a major city track at the foot of the cathedral. Turn right on this, and left further on to reach the cathedral

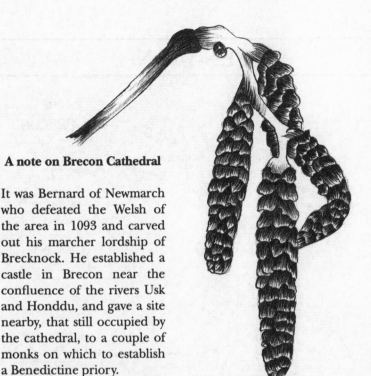

A note on Brecon Cathedral

It was Bernard of Newmarch who defeated the Welsh of the area in 1093 and carved out his marcher lordship of Brecknock. He established a castle in Brecon near the confluence of the rivers Usk and Honddu, and gave a site nearby, that still occupied by the cathedral, to a couple of monks on which to establish a Benedictine priory.

The nave of this church was used for parish worship, and the eastern end by the monks. Over the years the church was substantially rebuilt, the chancel, tower and transepts from around 1200, the nave about a hundred years later. In the fourteenth century chapels were added to the transepts.

At the time of the Dissolution of the Monasteries, the priory was still quite small, with just four monks in addition to the prior himself, and fifteen servants. The church, already partly used by the parish, became in its entirety the parish church. The man who carriedout the inspection of the monastery of behalf of Henry VIII, ended up buying the other monastic buildings and converting the prior's house into his own home.

It was not until 1923 that the building became a cathedral, at the centre of the newly formed doicese of Brecon and Swansea. With this decision came further restoration, building on that carried out under the supervision of Sir Gilbert Scott in the latter half of the nineteenth century.

PEN-Y-FAN

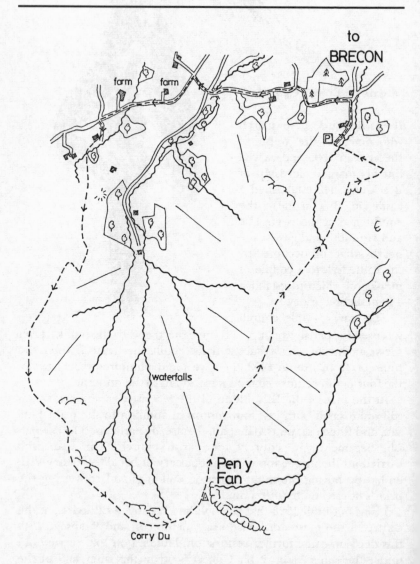

Two and a half hours. (That is pure walking time at a fairly steady pace, so add on additional time if likely to travel slower, and wanting to stop often to admire the views and catch your breath!)

Pen-y-Fan is one of the most spectacular places in the U.K. I have tried to pick a route which is not so well trodden as some. Even so the paths are largely well formed, though some are quite narrow at times. There is also a section of pretty quiet minor road at the foot of the beacons. Unsurprisingly, there are wide views to be had, though those with less of a head for heights shouldn't stray too close to the edge near the summits. The hills are bleak, so extra care should be taken on this walk to ensure footwear with a good grip, and even if it appears a quiet, windless day in the valleys, it can be quite different on the ridges at the top. The route described is about as gentle as can be for the ascent, breaking the back of it in two main bursts, the last seeming and probably is the most severe. But you can catch your breath on the intervening fairly flat stretch! Bear in mind, you will be clambering up some 630metres of hillside in height alone.

From the centre of Brecon take the road signposted to Landovery, this leading over a bridge across the Usk. You soon reach a church on the left, and you want to take the road to the left a few hundred yards beyond the church, the road named Ffrwdgrech Road. Carry on along this and it presently comes to a three-way fork, where you bear left to Cwm Gwdi army training camp. This is a very narrow road so beware, and you keep on it till you come to the entrance to the camp straight ahead. Carry on ahead and over the cattle grid and the road passes the army camp and reaches a car park, where you can park.

Walk back down the road past the camp and over the cattle grid, turning left when you reach the junction with the road. Follow this along and turn left at the road junction you come to. Keep on along the road, passing a lane off to the left, and you cross a bridge (with a little waterfall on your right) and then rise to a staggered crossroads. Go straight over this and you soon come to a second crossroads. This time turn left, passing two entrances to farms on your right, after which you come to a junction with another road. Here you turn left, and almost immediately left again up a track.

This leads you past a house, and you continue on the main track following the stream on your left. (Ignore the stile on the far side of the stream almost opposite the end of the buildings.) Soon your track will cross the stream and enter onto the open hillside by a gate.

Ahead of you you can see the old sunken remains of a track, and you want to follow this up the hillside. Over the first ridge the path becomes less clear, but you aim for the left-hand end of the limb of the beacons towards which you are heading, continuing in fact on much the same sort of line on which you've been walking. (Your path is not the one that seems to go straight up the end of the hill, your's has a more gentle zig-zag!) As you near the hill you will probably make out much more distinctly the line of your path, which bears left and up across the flank of the hill.

When you reach this part of the path, you are about to start the first major part of the ascent. The path leads along the flank of the hill, then bends right and fairly presently afterwards, left once more. To take your mind off the climb, keep an eye out for the waterfalls on the stream in the valley to your left. The path slowly becomes less steep as it emerges towards the top of the shoulder of the hill. It can become more indistinct further on, but if in any doubt, it stays close to the top of the shoulder, but slightly to its left if anything. This can be a benefit in windier weather as at least you gain some shelter.

As you round the bluff on your left you will reach an obelisk marking the spot where the remains of a child were found who had gone missing on the Beacons in August 1900. If you haven't already, it's worth taking a step close to the edge on your left and seeing the little tarn below you.

Your path carries on along the ridge, soon to start the last major ascent. Do keep to the path that's partially been created by the National Trust—if you walk to either side of it you're only likely to increase the erosion which they're trying to prevent. At the top you will have climbed Corry Du, Pen-y-Fan is the next peak over.

Technically the path turns right away from Corry Du and Pen-y-Fan, whence you will join a path off to your left taking you to the higher summit. Buit another path appears to have been formed linking the two.

From Pen-y-Fan you take the left-hand ridge (the slightly more inviting looking one for those without a head for heights), and have an initial steep descent before you join a flatter path along the crest of the ridge. You are now walking down the other side of the valley to that which you walked up. The path even rises a touch at the end of this first run, before dropping down to another knoll. From this knoll you can either keep to the main track which will lead you back to the car park, or take a definitive footpath to approach the car park from the other side of the valley.

If you choose the latter route (as shown on the map), from this knoll you need initially to keep close to the right hand ridge, before

picking up a path which leads down around the inside flank of the little valley. This path becomes steeper as it descends the hill, and will swing round the hill to make it seem as if you are diverging from the car park and army camp. Well, you are, and you need to keep the position of the car park fixed in your mind as it disappears below tree height. You will reach some upright marker posts stuck in the ground on your left, where you turn left and slither down the last part of the hill. Then walk along the main path you come to for some forty yards, before heading half-right in the direction of the car park. There is no obvious path, you have to skirt around trees and gorse bushes. If your memory has held good you will come to the stream at a point immediately above a bridge. Cross the bridge, go over the stile ahead and the path on the far side will lead you out just below the car park.